The Media Economy

The Media Economy analyzes the media industries and their activities from macro- to micro-levels, using concepts and theories to demonstrate the role the media plays in the economy as a whole. Representing a rapidly changing and evolving environment, this text breaks new ground through its analysis from two unique perspectives:

- examining the media industries from a holistic perspective by analyzing how they function across different levels of society (global, national, household, and individual);
- looking at the key forces (technology, globalization, regulation, and social aspects) constantly evolving and influencing the media industries.

It includes examples from both developed and developing nations, as well as data and trends from these countries, offering a broad arena of study.

Key features of this innovative text include:

- topics new to media economics texts, such as finance and investment, labor, and social aspects;
- accessible discussion of complicated concepts and their application to media industries;
- new directions for both theoretical and methodological areas.

With the media industries in an ongoing state of change and transformation, *The Media Economy* offers new reference points for the field to consider when defining and analyzing media markets. It will be essential reading for students and practitioners in media management and economics who need to understand the role of media in the global economy.

Alan B. Albarran is professor of radio, television, and film and the director of the Center for Spanish Language Media at the University of North Texas. He has extensive experience as an editor and author and is widely recognized as an international scholar in the area of media management and economics. He is former editor of the *Journal of Media Economics* and the *International Journal for Media Management*.

MEDIA MANAGEMENT AND ECONOMICS SERIES

Albarran, **The Media Economy**

Albarran/Olmstedd/Wirth, **Handbook of Media Management and Economics**

Ha/Ganahl, **Webcasting Worldwide: Business Models of an Emerging Global Medium**

The Media Economy

Alan B. Albarran

Routledge
Taylor & Francis Group

NEW YORK AND LONDON

First published 2010
by Routledge
711 Third Avenue, New York, NY 10017

Simultaneously published in the UK
by Routledge
2 Park Square, Milton Park, Abingdon, Oxon OX14 4RN

Routledge is an imprint of the Taylor & Francis Group, an informa business

© 2010 Taylor & Francis

Typeset in Sabon by Swales & Willis Ltd, Exeter, Devon

Library of Congress Cataloging in Publication Data
Albarran, Alan B.
The media economy / Alan B. Albarran.
p. cm
Includes bibliographical references and index.
1. Mass media–Economic aspects. I. Title.
P96.E25.A483 2010
338.4'730223–dc22
2010011613

ISBN 10: 0–415–99045–9 (hbk)
ISBN 10: 0–415–99046–7 (pbk)
ISBN 10: 0–203–92771–0 (ebk)

ISBN 13: 978–0–415–99045–5 (hbk)
ISBN 13: 978–0–415–99046–2 (pbk)
ISBN 13: 978–0–203–92771–7 (ebk)

This book is dedicated to Dr. John W. Dimmick, my mentor, fellow researcher, and friend. Thanks for everything.

CONTENTS

PREFACE

The Media Economy is an attempt to look at the study of media economics from a 21st-century perspective, utilizing a holistic view. In the initial decades of inquiry (circa 1950s to the 1990s) media economics tended to be approached from singular viewpoints—such as focusing on particular media industries, or specific practices like financing and economics, or a particular country, like the United States. Much of my earlier work and books on the subject fell into this same paradigm. My research and writing reflected what others were writing and researching.

Clearly the media industries (and for that matter much of the world) have experienced unprecedented change and evolution since 1990 owing to a confluence of factors: globalization, regulatory reform, social changes, and of course technology. This has forced researchers in the field of media economics to take a wider viewpoint in an attempt to assess what is happening. The result is clear—media economics must be examined across a broader spectrum of inquiry, because it cuts across numerous areas and levels of activity.

The Media Economy will hopefully break new ground in the way media economics is both studied and approached by students, scholars, researchers, and policymakers. *The Media Economy* is a broader title that reflects the holistic nature of the field of study. This text will emphasize the key drivers and concepts associated with the media economy, and the relevant theories and application of these theories to analyze the media economy. The book draws on examples from around the globe as well as from the United States to illustrate key points and concepts.

THE PLAN OF THE BOOK

This book is designed for both research and teaching purposes. For researchers, this book provides a tool to understand the different components of the media economy and their influence on one another. As a teaching tool this book could be used as a primary text or a secondary text at both the undergraduate and the graduate level for courses in such subjects as media economics or media management, or a seminar in media industries. My goal as a writer is to communicate ideas as clearly as possible, so the style is designed to be clear and concise.

There are a total of 12 chapters in the book, and there are learning objectives found at the beginning of each chapter and discussion questions at the end of each chapter. The first four chapters provide an introduction and foundation for analyzing the media economy and introducing theories and concepts along with a discussion of markets and their evolution. Chapters 5–9 look at the main drivers of the media economy, including technology, globalization, regulation, and social aspects. Chapter 10 is devoted to finance, valuation, and investment, and Chapter 11 examines labor in the media economy. Chapter 12 concludes with a summary and directions for future research.

ACKNOWLEDGEMENTS

This book took the longest of any project I have worked on in my career. That was never my intention. *The Media Economy* was originally due to be published in 2009, but a series of personal events delayed the completion of this work until late in 2009. During a span of 18 months (April 2008 to July 2009) my wife Beverly and I lost both of our mothers, and my wife also lost her twin brother. We suffered the loss of a dear family pet as well. Our faith in God nurtured us and sustained us during the sad times, along with the support of family, friends, and one another, but it did take a toll on my writing and research.

As such, I deeply appreciate my professional relationship and friendship with Linda Bathgate, my editor at Taylor & Francis/ Routledge, for her understanding and empathy in giving me time to complete this project. Linda, all I can say is "Thank you." I also greatly appreciate Linda's assistant Katherine "Kate" Ghezzi, for her attention to any questions or other needs I had as an author in working on this book and other projects.

I thank my friend Dr. David H. Goff at the University of North Florida for reviewing several chapters of the book and offering important suggestions. I deeply appreciate the support of administrators at the

University of North Texas, especially Department of Radio, Television and Film chair Melinda Levin, for granting me a faculty development leave during the fall of 2008 to work on this project and another book completed during this time, *The Handbook of Spanish Language Media*. At UNT, master's candidate and research assistant Brian Hutton was helpful in finding and updating data in several chapters to help finish this project. I also want to acknowledge the assistance of a former UNT colleague, Dr. Fang Liu (now Dr. Allison Fang Scott), who contributed to earlier drafts of two chapters in this book.

Last but certainly not least, I want to thank my wife and soulmate Beverly for her constant love and unwavering support while I worked through yet another book project.

Alan B. Albarran
The University of North Texas
December 2009

CHAPTER 1

Understanding the Media Economy

In this chapter you will learn:

- how to define the media economy;
- the forces that impact the media economy;
- macroeconomic and microeconomic perspectives used to study the media economy;
- how the media industries influence a nation's gross domestic product.

INTRODUCTION

This book is an effort to understand how the media industries interact and interplay with one another and how they influence economic activity at different levels of society. In this sense, you may be wondering about the title of this book, and why it isn't called "media economics" or some variation of that name. The reason is the media economy is a much broader and more complicated topic. The title *The Media Economy* reflects the importance of the media as part of the economics of a nation, and the globe.

The study of the media economy needs to be approached from a holistic view. Historically, media economics has been examined using singular viewpoints—such as focusing on a particular media industry, or specific practices like financing, or a particular country, like the United States or the United Kingdom. Yet, because of globalization, regulatory reform, social changes, and technology, the study of media economics demands a wider viewpoint. Media economics must be examined across a broader spectrum of inquiry, as it cuts across numerous areas and levels of activity—hence the idea of a media economy.

This book is an examination of new directions in the field of media economics. The media industries are one of many drivers of the economy in most developed and developing nations. Further, the media is constantly changing and evolving. Increasing fragmentation and digitalization of the media industries have eliminated the boundaries associated with studying "traditional" media. Television, radio, and newspapers no longer operate as single entities, but as enterprises offering content across multiple distribution platforms.

A key goal of this book is to analyze the key drivers and concepts associated with the media economy, including the relevant theories (and application of these theories) across the media economy. In order to define the media economy, we must first have a basic working knowledge of economics.

A BRIEF LOOK AT THE STUDY OF ECONOMICS

Economics is a field of study that came of age in the 17th century. First known as political economy, eventually the area would be shortened to just the term "economics" by the beginning of the 20th century (Albarran, 2004).

Economics is built on the concepts of supply and demand. In its simplest form, suppliers create goods and services from limited resources to meet the wants and needs or demand of consumers. Applied to the media industries, suppliers consist of TV and radio stations, satellite networks, and print publications, to name a few. The actual goods and services are best thought of as content—whether consumed on a TV or a computer, or through a handheld device like a smart phone. Consumers are represented by two key constituencies: the actual audience that views, listens or reads content, and the advertisers who buy time and space in the media to reach consumers in order to sell products and services.

Economics is traditionally studied in terms of *macroeconomics* and *microeconomics* perspectives, and the field of media economics has tended to follow suit. Macroeconomics examines the whole economic system, and is usually studied at a national or even a global level. Macroeconomics includes topics such as economic growth indices (interest rates, money supply, job creation), political economy (broadly defined as public policies toward the economy), and national production and consumption measured by gross domestic product (GDP) and gross national product (GNP).

Microeconomics takes a more narrow view by examining the activities of specific aspects of the economic system, such as individual markets, firms, or consumers. Microeconomics examines topics like market structure, and firm conduct and behavior. There will be more discussion of these two dimensions throughout this book.

WHAT IS THE MEDIA ECONOMY?

Albarran (2002, p. 5) previously defined media economics as "the study of how media industries use scarce resources to produce content that is distributed among consumers in a society to satisfy various wants and needs." But, to define the media economy, a broader and more inclusive definition is warranted. Therefore, the *media economy* is defined as *the study of how media firms and industries function across different levels of activity* (e.g., global, national, household, and individual) *in tandem with other forces* (e.g., globalization, regulation, technology, and social aspects) *through the use of theories, concepts, and principles drawn from macroeconomic and microeconomic perspectives.*

Media Firms and Industries

Now, in order to provide a more complete understanding of this broad definition, let's break down the key components for further analysis, beginning with *media firms* and *industries*. Media firms represent individual companies or entities that are incorporated through their respective domestic country, that operate for a profit. Media firms can be publicly held firms (owned by stockholders or shareholders) or privately held firms (also owned by stakeholders but not listed on any stock exchange). Examples of publicly held media firms include large conglomerates such as Time Warner, Disney, Sony, and News Corporation, or companies that operate in only one or two media markets such as Gannett (publishing and television) or Saga Communications (radio). Privately held media firms include such companies as Bertelsmann, Univision, and Clear Channel.

Economists define an industry as a group of sellers offering the same or similar products. Companies that are engaged in cable television, like Comcast, Time Warner, and Cablevision, are members of the cable television industry. DirecTV and EchoStar (owner of the Dish Network) compete in the satellite industry. AT&T and Verizon are two leaders in the telecommunications industry, and also offer multichannel television services similar to cable and satellite known as IPTV, or Internet Protocol Television. Hence, a unique feature of the evolving media industries is the changing nature of their markets and industries. Companies now compete with one another across markets and in different industries in the media economy.

Levels of Activity

Another important aspect of the definition of the media economy is the word *levels*, used to describe where activity among media firms and industries actually takes place. For example, many large companies like Viacom, Disney, Time Warner, News Corporation, Bertelsmann, and Sony compete at a *global* level, offering their media products and services throughout the world. At the *national* level, companies focus on their domestic boundaries, and attempt to cover the entire country. Examples at the national level include the broadcast networks, satellite-delivered channels, and magazines.

The *household* level is where a great deal of media consumption takes place, but that too is evolving. Households have access to multiple devices or platforms capable of receiving content from a number of media firms and industries. These devices include television and radio receivers, DVD and DVR players, desktop and laptop computers, and wired (broadband) and wireless household networks. The concept of a household has also evolved, ranging from the traditional nuclear family to single parents and even single households. The household is important in the media economy, for tracking not only household media usage but also media-related expenditures and various subscriptions for media content. Further, a household's income level tells us a lot about general consumption patterns as part of the overall economy.

Finally, the *individual* level is becoming even more important in the media economy. Even in a traditional nuclear family household there are differences in the way parents use the media in comparison to their children, and how much time and attention each allocates to the media. All of us are limited to 168 hours in a week. How we choose to spend our time in media-related activities represents an economic action that economists refer to as *allocation*.

In the media economy, a growing trend is towards greater individual empowerment and opportunities for media consumption. Younger audiences who have grown up with the Internet and file-sharing are very comfortable watching content on a laptop screen or cell phone, while many older adults would prefer a traditional TV set or, better yet, a large-screen receiver. Mp3 players like the iPod offer playback of video and audio content that has been downloaded from the Internet or supplied by the user. Smart phones can surf the web, run applications, play music, take photos, and send messages/email, and they still make phone calls! Social networking sites like Facebook and MySpace allow friends to share intimate thoughts and feelings as well as media content with one another, and create "buzz" and awareness of new products and services. Twitter is another social networking site that has been embraced by both individuals and businesses. YouTube is just one of many services that allow users to share user-generated content with one another.

In the evolving media economy, the individual is in charge of his/her own media consumption—what you want, when you want it, and how you wish to access it. This seminal change has disrupted traditional business models (we discuss this trend throughout the text) and forced advertisers constantly to re-evaluate their strategies and marketing practices. Likewise, traditional media have had to evolve and respond so as not to be totally left out of the picture.

These levels of activity are constantly ongoing in the media economy. At any given moment, media firms are engaging consumers across all levels, but increasingly it is the individual level where the sea change has taken place. One huge challenge for media firms is how to develop as multi-platform entities that can reach consumers at all levels of activity. That in itself is a tremendous task, made all the more difficult by the fact that the media economy is impacted by other forces as well.

Other Forces

There are four other predominant forces that interact with economic aspects in any society that deserve discussion in the media economy. These forces are globalization, regulation, technology, and social aspects. Each of these forces is dealt with in more detail in individual chapters later in the text, so here I simply offer a brief introduction.

Globalization is a critical driver in the media economy. For media firms and industries, the act of globalization—a word with many different meanings—occurs when companies reach beyond domestic borders to engage consumers in other nations or markets. Originally, media globalization meant selling content around the world, a practice that first started with Hollywood films and expanded later to television programming. The United States is the largest exporter of media content in the world, leading to many concerns about the influence of America abroad and the notion of "cultural imperialism" (Jayakar & Waterman, 2000).

Globalization also occurs when companies acquire other properties in other countries. News Corporation began as an Australian newspaper company, acquiring newspapers in the United Kingdom and the United States, and later on purchasing a group of television stations that would eventually become the Fox TV Network. Sony entered the film industry by first acquiring Columbia Tristar and later MGM.

Yet another form of globalization occurs when a company establishes multiple locations in other nations. The Nielsen Company, a privately held firm specializing in various types of research services, operates in over 100 countries throughout the world. Disney operates theme parks in several important global cities, and also has a strategic base in Latin America. Bertelsmann, the global leader in book publishing, has operations around the world through its various publishing entities.

Regulation and regulatory practices differ from country to country. Through policy and regulation, governments require business and industry to follow certain rules and guidelines. Regardless of the country, most businesses and industry dislike being regulated and would prefer to operate without government oversight. But regulation is important in establishing and maintaining competition, to protect workers and consumers, and to generate revenues through taxation in order for a government to function.

Over the years the media industries have evolved in many developed nations from being strictly regulated to various forms of deregulation and liberalization. In the United States and United Kingdom, regulations for the media industries have been repeatedly relaxed since the 1980s, most notably in regard to media ownership. Other nations have followed suit to some degree, while in other regions of the world (e.g., the Middle East, Asia) heavier regulation exists.

Technology has both enhanced and disrupted the media economy. Innovations in technology with distribution and reception technologies continue at a rapid pace. The plethora of technological advances has forced media companies to try to keep up with one another, while at the same time not knowing what technologies consumers will ultimately adopt. The digital environment has disrupted traditional business models (Downes, 2009). In an analog world, content was controlled by media companies and access limited. In the digital world, these barriers are removed.

For media companies, finding new business models and revenue streams is a major priority in the media economy. For consumers, today's technological device is likely to be either limited or obsolete in just a few months, replaced by yet another innovation. But, overall, the benefits of technology for media companies and consumers in the media economy outweigh the negatives. Technology offers faster and easier tools to deliver and access entertainment and information. Technologies like the iPod, the DVR, and smart phone are just a few examples of popular consumer technologies.

Social aspects are also important in the media economy. The audience is no longer a mass entity, but an aggregate of many different demographic groups and lifestyles with different interests that evolve through the life cycle. The composition of the audience is changing almost on a daily basis. The baby boomer generation is graying and growing older; American society along with many other nations is becoming much more ethnically diverse and multicultural; people are living longer and working longer; younger people are more technologically savvy and prefer to access content differently than adults.

Given all the outlets available for entertainment and information in a digitally delivered media economy, audience fragmentation is at an all-time high. This is forcing media companies to place more emphasis on research in order to better understand their audiences for media content, and provide more accountability to advertisers. Audience members are more empowered than at any other time in media history. Audience members no longer just consume content—they can also make content in a multitude of ways, whether through blogging, podcasting, uploading videos, or social networking, to name a few options. Social aspects are yet another force driving change across the media economy.

Microeconomic and Macroeconomic Perspectives

The final part of our working definition for the media economy involves the application of theories, concepts, and principles involving *microeconomic* and *macroeconomic* perspectives. These perspectives were introduced earlier in this chapter, presenting the primary differences between the two theoretical dimensions.

Media economics research has traditionally oriented itself towards studies of individual firms and industries following a microeconomics perspective. In terms of published research, microeconomics has tended to dominate the field of inquiry. Macroeconomics has not received nearly as much scholarly interest despite the fact that we are increasingly living in an era of media globalization, where economic activity in one region of the world influences the others.

The remainder of this chapter attempts to answer one key research question, driven from a macroeconomics perspective: How important are the media industries to a nation's economy? This question centers on the national level. As this question is best addressed from a macroeconomics perspective, let's first investigate the existing body of literature on this topic.

MACROECONOMICS AND THE MEDIA INDUSTRIES

Macroeconomics was introduced earlier as an area concerned with many different topics, such as economic growth, employment trends, aggregate production and consumption, and inflation (Albarran, 2002). Macroeconomics became an important tool for governmental fiscal policy decisions in both Western Europe and the United States during the 1950s and 1960s, influenced by the work of John Maynard Keynes, the founder of the area known as Keynesian economics.

Keynes's most influential work was *The General Theory of Employment, Interest and Money* (1936), which provided a modern rationale for the use of government spending and taxation to stabilize an economy. Keynes argued governments would spend and decrease taxes when private spending was insufficient and fearing a recession; conversely, governments would reduce spending and increase taxes when private spending was too great and leading to the threat of inflation. Keynes's work, focusing on the factors that determine total spending, remains at the core of macroeconomic analysis. Keynes's theories and writings would receive new acclaim as a result of the devastating global financial crisis of 2008, which resulted in massive amounts of government stimulus and liquidity to revive a global economy in deep distress.

Other scholars helped refine macroeconomics through their own research investigating related topics in the field (see Ekelund & Hebert, 1990). These include Irving Fisher (money, prices, and statistical analysis), Knut Wicksell (public choice), A. C. Pigou (welfare economics), and Milton Friedman (economic policy and consumption). In the 21st century, macroeconomics has broadened in its inquiry to be concerned with topics like international economics, better methods of applied economics, and the enhancement of powerful analytical and statistical tools through econometric analysis.

In applying macroeconomic analysis to the media industries, the literature is sparse with the exception of policy and regulatory analysis. Policy studies typically attempt to analyze the impact of specific regulatory actions on existing markets and industries. For example, Bates and Chambers (1999) considered the economic impact of radio deregulation, Ford and Jackson (2000) examined policy decisions in U.S. cable television, and Lutzhöft and Machill (1999) reviewed how regulation impacted French cable systems. Owers, Carveth, and Alexander (2004) examined macroeconomic concepts and their application to the media industries. In terms of employment, two studies offer descriptive analyses of labor trends in selected media industries (see Albarran, 2008; Harwood, 1989).

In terms of national studies, Collins and Litman (1984) compared the differences in program offerings and development between the Canadian cable industry and the U.S. cable industry, and concluded that a different economic status in each country, cultural peculiarities, and contrasting theories of regulation contributed to the differences. Goff (2002) reviewed broadband strategies of telecommunications operators in the United Kingdom, Spain, France, and Germany. Jung (2004) examined how U.S. advertising agencies entered foreign markets using acquisitions or joint ventures. Lee and Chan-Olmsted (2004) investigated the factors that have led to the differences in the development of broadband Internet in South Korea and the United States. Fan (2005) examined the regulatory factors that have affected the availability and affordability of Internet access in China and Australia. Sohn (2005) compared satellite broadcasting among the United States, Japan, the United Kingdom, and France.

Hence, this review confirms that the literature base for the application of macroeconomics concepts to the media industries is sparse. The remainder of this chapter utilizes a case study approach to look at several different countries using macroeconomic concepts to determine the relative importance of the media industries to a country's economy.

THE GROUP OF 20 NATIONS

For this analysis a number of different macroeconomic concepts and variables drawn from several different sources were used to analyze the key economic countries making up the Group of 20 nations. The G-20 nations were formed in 1999, increasing from the original G-7 nations (Canada, France, Germany, Italy, Japan, the United Kingdom, and the United States). The G-7 was originally formed to foster cooperation on economic issues among the world's leading industrialized countries. By 1999, wide recognition of the importance of the global economy led to the addition of new members to form the G-20 (*About G-20*, n.d.). The countries joining in 1999 included Argentina, Australia, Brazil, China, India, Indonesia, Mexico, Russia, Saudi Arabia, South Africa, South Korea, Turkey, and the European Union. However, for the analysis presented in this chapter, the European Union was omitted from further review owing to its unique status as a member of the G-20 but not a single nation.

To begin this analysis, two data sources were consulted to understand how the media influence GDP. The Central Intelligence Agency (CIA) *World Factbook* (2009a) provides data on every country in the world, especially descriptive data and statistics. The publication *Datamonitor* is an excellent source that publishes an annual profile of the media industries on 15 of the G-20 nations. *Datamonitor* defines the media as the advertising, broadcasting and cable TV, publishing, movies, and entertainment markets, but it does not include the telecommunications sector.

Economic Variables

Data on GDP, GDP growth rate, and GDP per capita, as well as the country's inflation and unemployment rates, were analyzed to detail the economic position of each country included in this study. Information on these macroeconomic variables was collected for the year 2008 from the CIA *World Factbook* (2009a).

In the CIA *World Factbook* (2009a), GDP is defined as "the gross domestic product or value of all final goods and services produced within a nation in a given year." GDP growth rate is defined as "GDP growth on an annual basis adjusted for inflation and expressed as a percent." GDP per capita is defined as "GDP on a purchasing power parity basis divided by population as of 1 July for the same year." The inflation rate contains "the annual percent change in consumer prices compared with the previous year's consumer prices," while the unemployment rate measures "the percent of the labor force that is without jobs."

Table 1.1 compares the G-20 nations in terms of the macroeconomic variables for the year 2008. As seen in Table 1.1, the United States had the world's largest economy in 2008 at $14.26 trillion, followed by China ($7.97 trillion), Japan ($4.33 trillion), India ($3.3 trillion), and Germany ($2.92 trillion). Other countries outside of the top five had GDP values ranging from Russia's $2.27 trillion to South Africa's $0.49 trillion.

China had the highest GDP growth rate at 9% among the nations, while Italy had the lowest at a negative 1.0%. In terms of GDP per capita, we find a much different picture, as the top five countries in this category are the United States, Canada, Australia, the United Kingdom, and Germany. China, Indonesia, and India all rank in the bottom three in terms of GDP per capita. Inflation is the highest in Russia, South Africa, and Turkey, while unemployment is the highest in South Africa, Saudi Arabia, and Turkey.

Table 1.1 Economic Variables Among the G-20 Nations, 2008

COUNTRY	GDP (TRILLIONS/ USD)	GDP GROWTH (%)	GDP PER CAP (USD)	INFLATION (%)	UNEMPLOYMENT (%)
Canada	$1.30	0.4	$39,100	2.4	6.2
France	$2.13	0.3	$33,200	2.8	7.4
Germany	$2.92	1.0	$35,400	2.7	7.8
Italy	$1.82	−1.0	$31,300	3.4	6.8
Japan	$4.33	−0.7	$34,000	1.4	4.0
Russia	$2.27	5.6	$16,100	14.1	6.4
UK	$2.23	0.7	$36,500	3.6	5.6
USA	$14.26	1.1	$46,900	3.8	7.2
China	$7.97	9.0	$6,000	5.9	4.0
Brazil	$1.99	5.1	$10,200	5.7	7.9
Mexico	$1.56	1.3	$14,200	5.1	4.0
Argentina	$0.57	6.8	$14,200	8.6	7.9
Australia	$0.80	2.3	$38,100	4.4	4.2
India	$3.30	7.4	$2,900	8.3	6.8
Indonesia	$0.91	6.1	$3,900	9.9	8.4
Saudi Arabia	$0.58	4.2	$20,500	9.9	11.8
South Africa	$0.49	3.1	$10,100	11.3	22.9
South Korea	$1.33	2.2	$27,600	4.7	3.2
Turkey	$0.90	1.1	$11,900	10.4	10.7

Source: CIA (2009a).

A Closer Look at the Top Five Nations

Let's examine the top five nations among the G-20 ranked by GDP by focusing on their media industries, starting with the United States. The U.S. media generated total revenues of $379.3 billion in 2008, making the U.S. the largest contributor to the global media market at 40.4% of total media revenues (Datamonitor, 2008e). The U.S. media industry maintained a compound annual growth rate (CAGR) of 2.5% in the five-year period of 2004–2008. The publishing sector was the largest U.S. media industry in 2008 at $157.5 billion, accounting for about 41.5% of the total media revenue in the United States in 2008 (Datamonitor, 2008e). Leading media companies based in the U.S. include Time Warner, Walt Disney, Comcast, News Corporation, and NBC Universal, which is expected to merge with Comcast.

China has the second-largest economy in the world based on GDP.

The Chinese media industry generated total revenues of $59.8 billion in 2008, while growing at a very strong CAGR of 11.9% in the five-year period of 2004–2008 (Datamonitor, 2008a). The publishing industry is the largest Chinese media industry, accounting for 52.7% of total media revenues at $31.5 billion (Datamonitor, 2008a). The leading Chinese media companies include People's Daily Group and China Central Television.

Japan has the third-largest economy in the world based on GDP (CIA, 2009a). The Japanese media industry generated total revenues of $95.2 billion in 2008 (Datamonitor, 2008d). The Japanese media industry experienced a slow growth rate of 108% in the five-year period of 2004–2008. The publishing industry is the largest media industry, accounting for 40.7% of the total media revenue in Japan in 2008 (Datamonitor, 2008d). Sony is the largest media company based in Japan, along with the video game maker Nintendo.

India is the fourth-largest county in terms of GDP at $3.3 trillion (CIA, 2009a). The Indian media industry generated total revenues of $16.7 billion in 2008 (Datamonitor, 2008c). India's media industries grew at a CAGR of 10.1% from 2004 to 2008. The publishing industry is the largest media industry at $6.4 billion, or 38.12% of total media revenues (Datamonitor, 2008c). Key companies include the Times Group, New Delhi Television, and Zee TV.

Germany has the largest economy in Europe and ranks fifth among the G-20 in GDP (CIA, 2009a). The German media industry generated total revenues of $63.5 billion in 2008. The German media industry experienced a nearly flat growth rate with a CAGR of 0.6% from 2004 to 2008. The publishing industry is also the largest media industry at $38.9 billion, or 61.2% of total media revenues (Datamonitor, 2008b). Bertelsmann and Axel Springer are two of the largest media companies based in Germany.

Media and Communication Data

Now let's examine the media- and communication-related variables in these nations. These variables provide indicators of the availability and development of the media industries in each country. Data was collected on: 1) the number of land phones, mobile phones, AM and FM radio stations, TV stations, and Internet users; and 2) media revenue variables, including the media revenue of a nation, which contains revenues of the advertising, broadcast and cable television, publishing, and movies and entertainment markets within a nation in a given year, and media revenue as a percentage of GDP of a nation. The two media revenue variables indicate the importance of the media industries to a nation's economy in absolute value and relative value, respectively.

Media and communication variables in each country as of 2008 are presented in Table 1.2. Among the nations, China had the most land phones, mobile phones, and Internet users; the United States had the most AM and FM radio stations; and Russia had the most TV stations (the majority of which are repeater stations owing to the geography). Although population of these nations and other factors should be taken into consideration when interpreting these data, they provide a picture of the media and communications infrastructure in these nations.

Table 1.2   Media and Communications in the G-20 Nations (2008)

COUNTRY	LAND PHONES (IN MILLIONS)	MOBILE PHONES (IN MILLIONS)	AM	FM	TV	INTERNET USERS (IN MILLIONS)
Canada	18.25	21.5	245	582	148	28.0
France	35.9	59.3	41	3,500	584	31.3
Germany	51.5	107.3	51	787	373	42.5
Italy	20.0	88.6	100	4,600	358	32.0
Japan	47.6	110.4	215	89	211	88.1
Russia	44.2	187.5	323	1,500	7,306[a]	30.0
UK	33.2	75.6	206	696	940	40.2
USA	150.0	270.0	4,789	8,961	2,218	223.0
China	365.6	634.0	369	259	3,240	253.0
Brazil	41.1	150.6	1,365	296	138	50.0
Mexico	20.5	75.3	850	545	236	22.8
Argentina	9.6	46.5	260	1,000[b]	42	9.3
Australia	9.4	22.1	262	345	104	11.1
India	37.5	427.3	153	91	562	80
Indonesia	30.4	140.6	678	43	54	13
Saudi Arabia	4.1	36	43	31	117	6.2
South Africa	4.4	45	14	347	556	5.1
South Korea	21.3	45.6	96	322	57	35.6
Turkey	17.5	65.8	16	107	635	13.1

a Includes repeater stations; not all unique TV stations.
b Estimated based on several sources.

Source: CIA (2009a).

Media Revenues' Influence on GDP

Media revenue as a percentage of GDP was calculated for each nation to answer the primary question of the influence of the media industries on a nation's economy. Information on media revenue was collected from Datamonitor's media industry profile reports of the nations included in this study. Table 1.3 shows information on media revenue, GDP, and media revenue as a percentage of GDP. Overall, media revenue accounted for a varying percentage of a nation's GDP, ranging from a low of 0.51% in India to a high of 2.73% in the United Kingdom. Media industry GDP represents a larger percentage among the original G-7 nations.

To drill down this data a bit, the United States is used as an example in Table 1.4 to illustrate how the importance of the country's media industries to the national economy has changed over the past 30 years by expanding previous research conducted by Waterman (2000).

Table 1.3   Media Revenue as a Percentage of GDP

COUNTRY	MEDIA REVENUE (BILLIONS/USD)	GDP (TRILLIONS/USD)	MEDIA AS A PERCENTAGE OF GDP
Canada	19.4	1.30	1.49
France	38.4	2.13	1.80
Germany	63.5	2.92	2.17
Italy	29.5	1.82	1.61
Japan	95.2	4.33	2.20
Russia	15.7	2.27	0.69
UK	61.0	2.23	2.73
USA	379.3	14.26	2.66
China	59.8	7.97	0.75
Brazil	18.6	1.99	0.93
Mexico	12.3	1.56	0.78
Argentina	N/A	0.57	N/A
Australia	13.3	0.80	1.66
India	16.7	3.30	0.51
Indonesia	N/A	0.91	N/A
Saudi Arabia	N/A	0.58	N/A
South Africa	N/A	0.49	N/A
South Korea	24.1	1.33	1.81
Turkey	N/A	0.90	N/A

Note: N/A means data on media revenues not available.

Sources: CIA (2009a); Datamonitor (2008a, 2008b, 2008c, 2008d, 2008e).

Table 1.4   Revenues of Mass Media Industries (Billions/USD), 1977–2008

	1977	1987	1998	2008
Broadcast TV	7.6	22.6	39.2	46.4
Cable and satellite TV	1.2	12.6	49.0	117.6
Home video rental/sales		5.7	16.9	22.4
Movie theaters	2.4	4.3	7.0	9.8
Radio	2.6	7.2	15.1	19.5
Newspapers	13.5	37.4	54.0	34.7
Magazines	4.0	10.5	20.4	33.5
Books	5.1	11.7	23.0	25.0
Records	3.5	5.0	13.7	8.5
Internet			12.6	23.4
Total	**39.9**	**117.0**	**250.9**	**379.3***

Growth rate of media revenue:

1977–1986: 193%

1986–1998: 114%

1998–2008: 51%

U.S. 2008 GDP	$2,031.4	$4,742.5	$8,759.9	$14,260.0
Total media as a percentage of U.S. GDP	1.96%	2.47%	2.86%	2.66%

* The U.S. total media revenue reported by Datamonitor (2008e) is $379.3 billion. There is a discrepancy of $38.5 billion in verifying the amount from the individual industries and trade associations. Most of this discrepancy is due to reporting in the publishing sector; Datamonitor reports $157.5 billion in publishing, while the various trade associations listed revenues at $93.2 billion. For consistency, the Datamonitor figure is used in Table 1.4.

Sources: Data for 1977–1998 are adapted from Waterman (2000). Data for 2008 are from the following sources: Association of American Publishers (2008); CIA (2009a); Entertainment Merchant Association (2009); Hoover's (2009a, 2009b); Interactive Advertising Bureau (2009a); Magazine Publishers of America (2009); Motion Picture Association of America (2009); National Cable & Telecommunications Association (2009); Newspaper Association of America (2009a); Radio Advertising Bureau (2009); Recording Industry Association of America (2009); Television Bureau of Advertising (2009); U.S. Census Bureau (2008).

In the United States, the media revenue/GDP ratio increased from 1.96% in 1977 to 2.86% in 1998. However, while absolute media revenues increased from $250.9 billion in 1998 to $379.3 billion in 2008, the media revenue/GDP ratio decreased from 2.86% to 2.66% over the same period. The growth rate of the U.S. media industries has been decreasing over time; it was 193% over the period of 1977–1986, 114% over the period of 1986–1998, and 51% over the period of 1998–2008.

One interesting note about the U.S. media data presented in Table 1.4 is that all areas of the media industry show growing revenues over the time periods examined with the exception of newspapers and records (music), which declined. This is not surprising for newspapers, given the loss of circulation, or for music, given the growth of digital distribution and the impact of piracy on the recording industry's traditional business model. Another observation is the relatively flat growth in other sectors such as books and movie theaters, and exceptionally strong growth in cable and satellite TV and the Internet, the latter of which tripled from the previous time period.

CONCLUSIONS

This macroeconomic analysis of the G-20 nations reveals that the media industries contribute over 2% of GDP in four countries, over 1% in five countries, and less than 1% in the remaining countries where data could be obtained. The United States has the largest GDP and the largest aggregate media revenues, but ranks second in terms of media contribution to GDP at 2.66% in 2008. The United Kingdom ranked first in terms of media/GDP at 2.74%, while Japan ranks third at 2.20%. At the other end of the spectrum, India had the lowest media/GDP ratio at 0.51%, with Russia (0.69%) and China (0.75%) rounding out the bottom three where data is available.

As for the relative importance of specific media industries across nations, the two largest media industries in terms of revenue are the publishing industry and the television (broadcast and cable television) industry. It indicates the importance of these two industries to a nation's media economy. In most cases, these areas combined contribute well over 50% to a nation's media revenue; in some cases, they account for even higher percentages. For example, publishing and television accounted for nearly 85.2% of the total media revenue in Germany in 2008 (Datamonitor, 2008b).

The media industries in the United States, the United Kingdom, and Japan are dominated by privately held companies; the opposite is true in countries such as Russia and China. Russia and China have openly embraced capitalism and are actively participating in the global economy, but the media systems in both countries remain state-controlled. No doubt, this is a contributing factor to their lower media revenues.

Interestingly, in the United States the 2.66% of media/GDP compares similarly to some other major categories in the country such as clothing (2.7% of GDP) and fuel (2.4%) (About.com: US economy, 2009). The $379 billion that represents the media sector in the United States is certainly an important contributor to the nation's GDP, and is valued similarly to other areas of consumption. But there is no question that there has been a slowdown in terms of media revenues over the time period examined. Based on these trends, one would expect to see continued growth in the media sector in the United States, but probably declining towards single-digit increases over the next ten years.

As for the other nations examined in this case study, one can certainly anticipate more rapid growth of media/GDP in the emerging economies of China, Mexico, and Brazil, while countries like Japan, the United Kingdom, Germany, and France will probably have similar experiences to the United States, in that we will see slower, incremental growth. Canada and Italy will follow suit, but at an even slower pace. China and Russia could explode in terms of media/GDP if more of their media industries were allowed to privatize through foreign investment. But these are political issues, and will require considerable change in both of these nations for their media/GDP to realize its true economic potential.

While this type of research is challenging given the lack of international data sources on media revenues, the analysis does illustrate the importance of media GDP to a nation's economy, and that the media sector (at least in the United States) is just as important as other key areas like clothing and fuel. While this analysis documents actual media GDP, it does not account for the broader influence of the media economy on consumer awareness, spending, and other economic and commerce activity. In that sense, the true influence of the media is much harder to gauge, and in reality is probably much larger for all nations.

SUMMARY

This chapter provides an introduction to the media economy and a case study of the G-20 nations to understand the importance of the media industries to a nation's economy. The media economy is the study of how media firms and industries function across different levels of activity in tandem with other forces through the use of theories, concepts, and principles drawn from macroeconomic and microeconomic perspectives.

Each segment of the media economy was broken down and defined, including the different levels of activity (e.g., global, national, household, and individual) and the impact of other forces (e.g., globalization, regulation, technology, and social aspects) on an economy. The chapter also explains the differences between macroeconomic and micro-economic perspectives, and how a combined approach offers better understanding of the media economy.

A case study of the G-20 nations using a macroeconomics perspective concluded the chapter, providing an analysis of economic variables, communication variables, media as a percentage of GDP, and a specific industry-by-industry assessment of the United States. In an examination of these countries, publishing and television are the two dominant sectors in terms of revenues, while other areas are experiencing slower growth. Other patterns were observed in comparing emerging economies to more established economies.

With this introduction complete, the next chapter in the text examines theories and approaches used in understanding the media economy using microeconomic, macroeconomic, and critical perspectives.

DISCUSSION QUESTIONS

1. Do you believe one level (global, national, household, and individual) of the media economy is more important than another to the media industries? Why or why not?
2. Of the forces impacting the media economy (globalization, regulation, technology, and social aspects), do you feel one has greater impact than the others? If so, which one and why?
3. How was the global recession and financial crisis in 2008 related to macroeconomics? What were some of the things governments tried to do to blunt the recession?
4. Since the media industries positively influence a nation's GDP, should governments invest more money in the media industries? Why or why not?
5. In the future, with all the media options and growing fragmentation among the audience, do you think the media industries will continue to have as big an impact on a nation's economy? Why or why not?

CHAPTER 2

Theories and Approaches Used to Examine the Media Economy

In this chapter you will learn:

- the three theoretical traditions used to understand the media economy;
- key theories and approaches used to analyze the media economy;
- the need for further refinement and development of theories to understand the media economy;
- the need for further refinement and development of methodological tools to evaluate and analyze the media economy.

In Chapter 1, the media economy was defined as *the study of how media firms and industries function across different levels of activity* (e.g., global, national, household, and individual) *in tandem with other forces* (e.g., globalization, regulation, technology, and social aspects) *through the use of theories, concepts, and principles drawn from macroeconomic and microeconomic perspectives*. This chapter focuses on the use of theories to help us understand the media economy.

Economics is considered a part of the social sciences, and in science theories are used to understand the relationship of different phenomena to one another. Theories are typically thought of as abstractions; a theory is not something tangible that you can pick up or hold. Theories are used in the sciences for many purposes, such as testing empirical observations, evaluation, and prediction. Theories are used to answer research questions, test a hypothesis, and build a base of knowledge about different phenomena.

Scholars or scientists share their knowledge and research on different theories through venues like conferences and symposiums, publications (books and scholarly journals), informal networks and learned societies, and the Internet. Theories form a backbone or foundation for every area of science. Theories help to organize a field of study, identify key concepts, understand patterns and trends, and clarify research assumptions.

The media economy is an abstraction. Therefore, we need to understand the theories we can use in order to understand how the media economy operates and functions in a social system. That is the goal and purpose of this chapter.

THEORETICAL TRADITIONS: AN INTRODUCTION

According to Picard (2006), media economics research has grown along three traditional paths: a theoretical tradition, an applied tradition, and a critical tradition, also known as the political economy of the media.

The theoretical tradition developed using many concepts and assumptions drawn from neoclassical economics, including micro-economics and macroeconomics perspectives. Neoclassical economics gained prominence in the 20th century as a vital area of study. Neoclassical economics is concerned with a number of topics, but at its core seeks to understand the interplay of supply and demand, prices, and quantity of production that functions in a market system, especially at the level of the firm.

The applied tradition examines topics revolving around the structure of various media industries and their markets. Applied research differs in that it is usually not built upon theoretical foundations. Examples of applied research would include industry-driven studies compiled by media-related associations, trade groups, consulting firms, and corporations. The applied tradition also embraces microeconomics and macroeconomics approaches. One drawback for scholars is that most of the research conducted in the applied tradition is proprietary in nature, meaning the results are not shared publicly.

The critical tradition lies in contrast to both the theoretical and the applied traditions. The critical tradition has a number of influences, ranging across Marxist approaches which view the media systems as a form of control of the ruling class over the working class, British cultural studies, research dealing with hegemony and power of the media, ownership studies, technological determinism, and social, cultural, and political concerns with the media.

A summary table of this brief discussion is provided in Table 2.1. These three traditions have resulted in a diverse set of theories available to researchers to study the media economy. It is important to understand

Table 2.1 Theoretical Traditions

TRADITION	INSTITUTIONAL FOUNDATIONS	LEVEL OF ANALYSIS	TOPICS EXAMINED
Theoretical	Neoclassical economics	Consumer, firm, market, industry	Supply, demand, price, production, elasticity, concentration, diversity
Applied	Industry-based Also influenced by neoclassical economics	Consumer, firm, market, industry	Structure, conduct, performance, spending, diversification, strategy
Critical	Marxist studies British cultural studies Political economy	Nation-state Global	Ownership, power, policy decisions, social and cultural effects of media, globalization, welfare

that no single tradition is the best one to use. It depends on the research questions being addressed or the hypotheses under study, which help determine the research tradition to use. If you are new to studying the media economy, embrace all three traditions as possible resources you can use in your investigation and analysis to provide the most complete understanding.

THE THEORETICAL AND APPLIED TRADITIONS
This section of the chapter examines the theories used in research on the media economy from the theoretical and applied traditions. The breadth of theory is quite extensive in these two areas; therefore the focus will be on the primary theories scholars have used to advance knowledge and development of the media economy.

The theories discussed below are used in conjunction with a variety of methodological approaches, depending on the type of study conducted and the availability of data and tools for analysis. In researching the media economy, it is best to use different methodological tools and techniques to address questions and hypotheses.

The Industrial Organizational (IO) Model
The industrial organizational model, also called the IO model, has been used by economists and researchers for many years to understand and analyze the relationships that exist between the structure, conduct, and

performance of a market across numerous industries. The model is also identified as the S-C-P model. The IO model was originally conceived by Bain (1959), and much of the early literature on media economics embraces it as a theoretical foundation because of its utility to researchers and its systematic approach to analyzing markets.

Researchers first examine the structure of the market with the IO model (Tirole, 1988). Five variables are commonly used to understand the structure of the market, including the number of buyers or sellers in a market, the differentiation among products offered in the market, the barriers to entry for new firms hoping to compete in the market, cost structures in the market, and the extent to which vertical integration exists in the market (Albarran, 2002).

In the IO approach, once market structure is identified, one of the common labels used to identify a market is attached—such as monopoly, duopoly, oligopoly, monopolistic competition, or perfect competition. These can be thought of as a continuum, where the number of sellers increases from one in a monopoly to an unlimited number in perfect competition.

Once the structure of a market is determined, researchers move to examine the conduct or behaviors exhibited by buyers and sellers in a market. Market conduct likewise involves five different variables for analysis in traditional IO studies: pricing policies, product strategy and advertising, research, investment, and legal tactics.

The last step in IO analysis involves a review of the performance of the market. In gauging performance, the emphasis is usually on financial indices, often in comparison to competitors in the same market or industry. The variables of efficiency, equity, and progress are used in IO analysis to study market performance.

Historically, the IO model offers great utility for media economics scholarship, examining markets from a microeconomics perspective. Some studies focus on just one part of the model, such as market structure (e.g., Bates, 1993; Wirth & Wollert, 1984), while others take a holistic approach, analyzing all parts of the model (Wirth & Bloch, 1995). The IO model has suffered criticism in that media economics scholarship relies too heavily on the IO model and that the IO model does not capture all of the challenges associated with studying new technologies and the convergence of markets. Still, it is an important part of the theoretical tradition flowing from a microeconomics orientation.

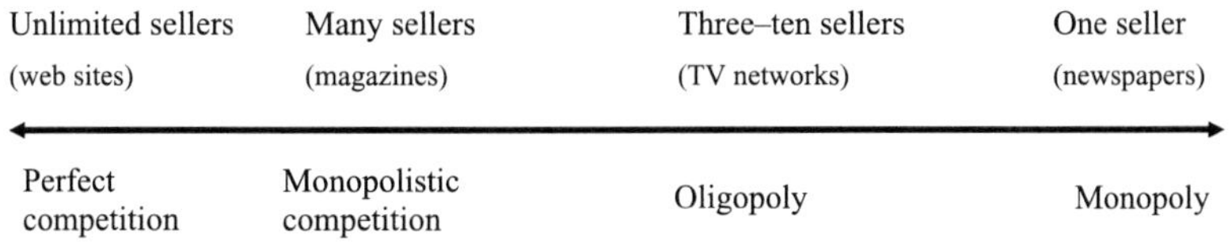

Unlimited sellers	Many sellers	Three–ten sellers	One seller
(web sites)	(magazines)	(TV networks)	(newspapers)

<-->

| Perfect competition | Monopolistic competition | Oligopoly | Monopoly |

Figure 2.1 The Theory of the Firm—Market Structure

Source: Author's compilation. In the theory of the firm, different market structures are determined based on several criteria, including the number of sellers in the market. Examples of media industries that correspond to the theory of the firm are listed above the continuum line in parentheses. Not shown is a duopoly, which would have only two sellers in a market.

The Theory of the Firm

Efforts to create a better understanding of market structure and refine the IO model led to the development of the theory of the firm. The theory of the firm is an expansion of the IO model, with the intent of gaining a more thorough understanding of the most common types of market structure: monopoly, oligopoly, monopolistic competition, and perfect competition. In most developed countries, media markets are dominated by oligopoly and monopolistic competitive structures (see Figure 2.1). Perfect competition is rarely found in the media industries (an exception being websites), while a monopoly structure tends to be limited to specific industries like newspapers and satellite radio.

The theory of the firm offers a parsimonious view of market structure. However, the whole notion of defining a market structure has become increasingly complicated owing to rapid consolidation across the media industries and technological convergence throughout the media economy. For example, does the market for radio include only broadcast radio? Or does it encompass a much wider approach to include HD and satellite radio, Internet radio, and podcasting? In the 21st-century media economy, market structure cannot clearly be defined using broad and simplistic labels. Further, there is so much blurring of markets that the theory of the firm has limited utility. However, the theory of the firm remains another theory in microeconomics that helped in the development of the field. More discussion on markets and how they are evolving in the media economy is presented in Chapter 4.

Relative Constancy

At the heart of the principle of relative constancy (PRC) is the desire to understand the relationship of consumer spending on media products and services. This research first debuted in the 1970s (McCombs, 1972) and posited that, on average, households over time spend around 3% of their disposable income on the "mass" media. The principle of relative constancy has been applied to many areas, including advertising, and has also been examined in a variety of cross-cultural contexts by examining spending in other countries (McCombs & Nolan, 1992). It is the primary theoretical approach to spending on the media found in media economics literature.

However, as our concept of mass media has diminished owing to audience fragmentation and a wider variety of choices, the idea of an average of 3% on media spending is questionable. Further, there are many more options for spending on media forms than when the PRC was first introduced. Does your monthly subscription to an Internet service provider count as media spending? What about buying a video game? Because the mobile phone is increasingly being used for media-related applications, does the monthly base subscription count as part of our media spending? These are questions that lack clarity in the emerging media economy.

Media Competition (and Coexistence)

The subject of how different media compete with one another has also been of interest to scholars of the media economy. Much of this literature on media competition draws upon the theory of the niche, which originated in the field of biology and the study of ecosystems (see Dimmick, 2003; Dimmick & Rothenbuhler, 1984). Niche theory seeks to understand how different species compete for scarce resources in order to survive. Originally used to study different populations of animals and extinction patterns, niche theory has been applied to the media industries by looking at how media companies compete for advertisers and audiences (analogous to scare resources) in order to gain competitive advantage over one another.

Niche theory quantifies competition among the media industries through a series of measures designed by Dimmick (2003). These include measuring the size or breadth of the niche of a competitor in a market. Other measures gauge the degree of overlap between competitors, and the superiority of one competitor to another. Niche theory has proven to be a valuable theoretical approach in media economics research.

Media competition studies typically take one of two forms: examining competition within an existing industry, or competition across media industries (see Albarran & Dimmick, 1996). One concern with niche theory is that we have established measures to determine within-industry competition, but lack sophisticated tools to measure across-industry competition, where in fact most large media conglomerates compete in the media economy.

Attention Economics

In the 1990s an area of research emerged based on the subject of attention, addressing how individuals manage the information they encounter. According to Davenport and Beck (2001, p. 20), "attention is focused mental engagement on a particular item of information. Items come into our awareness, we attend to a particular item, and then we decide whether to act." Lanham (2006, p. 6) adds that "there is too much information around to make sense of it all. Everywhere we look we find information overload." Napoli's (2003) examination of audience economics has a relationship to this area of study as well.

Iskold (2007) clarifies that *relevancy* is the key to understanding the attention economy, because it is the relevancy that individuals attach to information which encourages them to interact with content in the first place.

The idea of an "attention economy" or attention economics depending on which phrase one prefers is an area that is well suited for application to the media economy. While much of the research on the attention economy naturally focuses on the individual level, researchers could also examine the strategies media companies use to promote relevance among consumers, as well as how different types of content promote greater or lesser attention. In the busy, crowded, 21st-century media economy, the attention economy is one of the newer areas of inquiry where there is still much to learn.

Other Theories

There are numerous other theories that scholars utilize in studying the media economy, many of which are outgrowths or extensions of the IO model and neoclassical assumptions (Wildman, 2006). This section briefly examines some of the other theories that scholars have used in their research on the media economy.

Welfare economics is one of the oldest theories developed in neoclassical economics. Originally used to examine social policy and the economic decisions designed to improve conditions of society, welfare economics has also been used in analyzing media industries (see Busterna, 1988).

Behavioral economics is an area of study that attempts to understand the preferences and rational actions among economic firms or agents (Wildman, 2006). This area of study considers the psychological, social, and emotional factors used in making economic decisions, and their effect on pricing and allocation of resources.

Game theory utilizes a collection of mathematically driven models to analyze both the potential strategies and the possible outcomes of various interactions in a market. Game theory was popularized to some extent with the 2001 film *A Beautiful Mind*, based on the life of Nobel Prize winner and game theory innovator John Nash (1950).

Information economics considers the imperfection that exists among the level of information in a market system for economic firms or agents. This theory posits that information has value, and has particular application to the media industries if one considers that media content products and services are a form of information.

Finally, *transaction cost economics* attempts to identify the factors that make economic exchange risky, and to minimize the costs associated with such risks. This particular area of theory has wide application, and has been used in studying multiple industries and markets (Wildman, 2006).

Macroeconomic Approaches

In many countries, media industries function at the national level, enabling the use of macroeconomic approaches to the study of the media economy. As discussed in Chapter 1, there is a more limited body of literature involving macroeconomic analysis in the field of media economics, and we reviewed most of the literature related to macroeconomic approaches in the previous chapter. Here is a brief examination of the main areas of macroeconomic focus.

Policy studies attempts to analyze the impact of regulatory actions and decision-making on existing markets and industries (e.g., Bates & Chambers, 1999; Ford & Jackson, 2000; Lutzhöft & Machill, 1999). Because the media industries are regulated by governments, actions by policymakers impact markets in terms of their economic structure and potential, making this a natural area of inquiry.

Labor and employment is another area of study best approached from a macroeconomics perspective. Employment and labor trends help identify growth industries as well as those in decline. Employment directly impacts the economy of a nation, as lower employment tends to promote spending and consumption among consumers. Chapter 11 in this book looks deeper at the subject of labor and employment. Employment data in specific industries can be difficult to locate in some countries, making this area of research more challenging for media economy scholars.

Advertising trends are another important macroeconomic indicator of economic activity, and have been studied in many different ways (see Etayo & Hoyos, 2009; Picard, 2001). These types of studies build on aggregate data from specific industries or from countries and regions of the world to determine their overall economic impact.

The data from many government agencies and industry-driven studies have consistently shown that the bulk of advertising dollars are located in what is known as the triad, the regions of the world representing North America, Western Europe, and Japan and the Pacific Rim nations (Chan-Olmsted & Albarran, 1998). One global trend in advertising is the shifting of advertising dollars from traditional media outlets like newspapers and television to the Internet. Veronis Suhler Stevenson, in their *Communications Industry Forecast*, predicted that Internet advertising will be the largest category of advertising in the United States by 2011, totaling a projected $59 billion (Veronis Suhler Stevenson, 2008), with television second at $51 billion and newspapers in third place at $43 billion. Such shifts are taking place globally as well, as more and more advertisers invest more money in online advertising and other digital platforms.

THE POLITICAL ECONOMY TRADITION

As mentioned earlier in this chapter, the political economy tradition is driven by concerns regarding media power, hegemonic activities of dominant firms, and social and policy concerns. Contemporary political economy research is a critical form of scholarship, and is usually treated as a separate field of study in traditional media economics research.

In the development of this area of study, the political economy tradition is itself broad and diverse, emerging as a counter to positivist approaches driving much of mainstream economic theory. The mass media and its various media industries became a natural area of study for political economy researchers, drawing scholars from fields such as political science, sociology, and economics, as well as journalism and communications (e.g., Croteau & Hoynes, 2006). Some of the main areas of study in this tradition are briefly discussed below:

- *Marxist studies.* Among the influences on the political economy tradition are the writings of Karl Marx, especially *The Communist Manifesto* (Marx & Engels, 1955) and *Capital* (Marx, 1936). Marxism is a broad philosophy examined across many fields. Marxism is highly critical of capitalism and the power of the ruling class over the working class. Critical studies dealing with media power, concentration of ownership, and news and information decisions driven by capitalistic concerns rather than public values are often the product of a Marxist overview.

- *Hegemony* is concerned with the idea that a culture can be dominated or ruled by another class. Rooted in Marxism, hegemony was popularized by the Italian philosopher Antonio Gramsci, and has application to many fields of study. Hegemonic studies of the media are critical of the exportation of media content, especially from countries like the United States. Political economists argue that Western-oriented content promotes morals and values from outside the local culture and is disruptive to other societies.

- *Technological determinism* is founded in the belief that technology and technical forces impact history, as well as social and cultural values, usually to the detriment of society (Smith & Marx, 1994). The growth of communications technology (Ellul, 1964), via satellites, broadband networks, and the Internet, has no doubt "shrunk" the world, and at the same time resulted in concerns over the "digital divide," the idea that access to technology further separates people by class.

It should be noted that this brief examination of the critical tradition is not representative of the wide body of scholarly literature in this area. For more insights, readers are encouraged to consult Garnham (1990), Mosco (2009), and McChesney (2000) for a good introduction to research in this tradition.

DEVELOPING AND ENHANCING THEORIES FOR THE MEDIA ECONOMY

The theories examined in this chapter represent the mainstream approaches drawn from the theoretical, applied, and critical traditions used to study the media economy. As a body of work, these theories have helped to move this field of study forward and guide scholars in their research and inquiry.

However, the many forces impacting media markets in the 21st century challenge us to think in different ways and ultimately to develop new approaches and refine our theoretical assumptions. This is not to suggest that the theories identified here are no longer useful to scholars. Instead, we must draw on this existing body of knowledge in order to develop new theoretical approaches to studying the many complexities of the media economy.

This section considers how we might begin to develop and expand new theories to understand the media economy. This investigation is not designed to formulate a "grand" theory of the media economy, but to provide ideas for future study and investigation of the media economy.

Multiple Levels of Analysis

We know the media economy functions at many different levels of activity, as defined in Chapter 1. Our working definition of the media economy posits that activities take place at the following levels: global, national, household, and individual (see Figure 2.2). Yet we do not have theories that can investigate these multiple levels of activity; in fact, most of our theories concentrate on a single level as identified in the theories reviewed in this chapter.

This is not to suggest that all studies need to examine all of these levels simultaneously, but we must recognize that each level is interconnected with the others. We need to develop more research that reflects the multiple levels of activity in the media economy. For example, in every society around the world the Internet continues to change the way individuals work and play. This also impacts what happens in households, such as in the broad area of online shopping—which in turn influences commerce at the national level. One obvious impact of these lower-level activities is the shifting of advertising dollars to the Internet from traditional areas like newspapers, radio, and television.

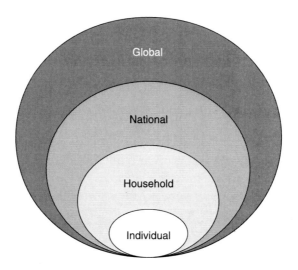

Figure 2.2 Multiple Levels of Analysis

Source: Author's rendition.

Globally, we see this shift of advertising dollars happening as well from traditional media to the Internet. Our research on the media economy needs to reflect these multiple levels of activity, and analyze and study these events.

By incorporating multiple levels of analysis into research designs, scholars will be able to obtain greater understanding and insight into the media economy with a holistic examination, as opposed to single examinations of one level of inquiry. This is an important first step in providing stronger theoretical work in the media economy—by examining multiple levels of analysis.

Redefining Markets and Market Structure

The intricacies of the media economy demand new definitions for markets and how we identify market structure. Media markets have historically been thought of in terms of "silos," such as the market for newspapers, the market for broadcast television, the market for cable television, and so forth. Yet the reality is that media companies are transforming themselves as multi-platform media enterprises (see Chapter 5), distributing content to different reception technologies available to consumers on a 24/7 basis. Future research must reflect this trend. Scholars need to take risks in offering new definitions for media-related markets, how to describe them, and most importantly how to research them.

As an example, in July of 2008, after about 400 days of waiting, the United States Federal Communications Commission (FCC) approved the merger of satellite radio companies Sirius and XM to become Sirius XM Radio. Critics of the merger argued that such a decision would create a monopoly; there would be only a single provider for satellite radio in America. XM and Sirius argued they competed in the market for audio entertainment and information, along with terrestrial radio, Mp3 players, and Internet radio. Ultimately, the FCC sided with Sirius XM that the market was much broader than simply satellite radio. Whether you agree with the FCC's decision or not, at the heart of this deliberation is the question of how to define a market.

Like our understanding of markets in general, our understanding of market structure must evolve as well. In our earlier discussion in this chapter on the theory of the firm, the problems were pointed out of using the abstract labels of oligopoly, monopolistic competition, and so on to define market structure. The problem is that the "old" labels still approach analysis from a single-market perspective, and do not account for activities across media markets. In defining traditional market

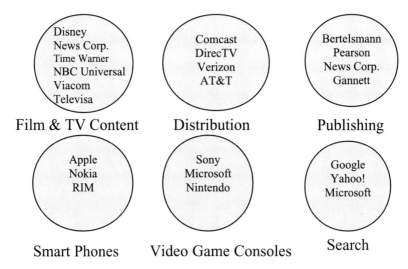

Figure 2.3   Designating Media Markets by Function

Note: Author's compilation.

structure, the first consideration involves understanding how many competitors exist in the market.

One solution may be to define media companies and their market structure by the activities they are engaged in rather than by the number of competitors. For example, it may be better to think of market structure in terms of the market for content, the market for distribution, the market for advertising, the market for smart phones, and so forth (see Figure 2.3). While this creates broader labels, it is more reflective of the reality of today's media economy. These ideas are expanded upon in Chapter 4.

New Theoretical Approaches and Refining Methodological Tools
Scholars in the media economy should consider new theoretical examinations using multiple methods of investigation. Considering the interplay of different business structures, government regulation, constant developments in new technology, and social policy implications across the media industries offers a unique opportunity to develop and explicate new theories and approaches. In order to accomplish this goal, researchers must be willing to move away from simply describing a specific industry structure and performance, take some risks, and generate more analytical and investigative analysis.

Ultimately, this means expanding methodological approaches used in the field. Improvements in developing theory must be realized in conjunction with enhancing our research methods and methodological tools. One particular area that deserves consideration is refining tools to measure concentration in media markets.

Concentration tools are useful only in measuring concentration within specific markets, but a number of large media companies engage in activities across many different markets. Disney, for example, is many things: a television company, a film company, the owner of many different cable channels like ESPN, theme parks, merchandising, and so on. Yet we have no concentration tools to gauge the influence of a company across different market segments. Albarran and Dimmick (1996) were among the first to identify this problem, and offered one descriptive solution to measuring across-industry concentration, but more work needs to be done. With so many media firms engaged simultaneously in different media markets, the development of tools to assess within-industry concentration is needed. Such measures would help us to understand other elements as well, such as competition and strategy formulation among media companies.

SUMMARY

Theories and theoretical development are critical in any field of study. In the media economy, theories are used to complement existing media and communication theories by adding important dimensions regarding the structure, conduct, and performance of media firms and industries, the interplay of economics, policy, and regulation, and audience behaviors and preferences.

The literature in the field of media economics has defined itself within three traditions: theoretical, applied, and critical. This chapter reviews the work in each of these three traditions. The chapter concentrates on introducing the reader to the theoretical and applied traditions.

Among the theories reviewed and analyzed in this chapter from the microeconomics dimension are: the industrial organization theory, also known as the IO model; the theory of the firm; the principle of relative constancy; media competition and coexistence; and attention economics. In addition, other theories were reviewed ranging from welfare economics to transaction costs economics. In examining the macroeconomic dimension of inquiry, the chapter reviews some of the literature related to policy studies, labor and employment, and advertising trends, along with some of the primary areas of study from the political economy tradition.

Together, these theories have provided tremendous help to scholars and policymakers in the development of the field and our understanding of the media economy. However, the rapid transformation and dramatic change accompanying the media industries in the 21st century calls for new areas of research and examination, and an expansion of existing theories.

The chapter suggests: that future research needs to explore multiple levels of analysis rather than the single dimensions that much of our previous scholarship has investigated; that researchers and policymakers must redefine rapidly changing and evolving media markets and take a new look at how markets are structured; and the need to develop better methodological tools, especially needed in areas like concentration analysis. This is not to attempt to create a new "grand" theory of the media economy, but rather to build and develop theories more suited to understanding the complex and rapidly changing environment that all levels of society are encountering across the media economy.

DISCUSSION QUESTIONS

1. How is theory used in the sciences? What questions are theories trying to answer?
2. There are three theoretical traditions used in studying the media economy. How does each of these areas contribute to our understanding of the media economy?
3. This chapter introduces you to a number of different theories and approaches used in the media economy. Which of these theories do you find the most useful and why?
4. The chapter suggests the field needs greater theoretical development. Why is this so? What are some of the challenges?
5. The chapter also suggests better methodological tools are needed as well as more theoretical development. Why do we need better methodological tools? What are some suggestions you have regarding new tools for analysis?

CHAPTER 3

Key Concepts to Understand the Media Economy

In this chapter you will learn:

- the different types of economies found around the globe;
- how to use the concepts of supply and demand, price, elasticity, and cross-elasticity to understand the functions of the media economy;
- the differences between wants, needs, utility, and value;
- how the concepts of allocation, vertical and horizontal integration, and competition and concentration are used in understanding the media economy.

This chapter introduces a number of the key concepts used to understand the media economy. While the "media economy" was defined in Chapter 1, here the focus is on recognizing the core concepts students, researchers, practitioners, and policymakers can utilize to understand exactly how the media economy functions.

While it would be helpful as the reader to have some prior knowledge of economics, this chapter offers a precise introduction to the most important concepts used in this text. For those without any background in economics, this chapter helps provide an important foundation for other chapters. Readers with a strong background in economics, especially microeconomics, can treat this chapter as a quick review, or move to other chapters to focus on the aspects of the media economy that are of the most interest. Further, the concepts introduced here are relevant to both macro- and microeconomics research and analysis.

TYPES OF ECONOMIES

The workings of an economic system are driven by the orientation of the government in which the economic system is found. The globe is a diverse place, made up of a wide variety of cultures and philosophies. The global economy is the aggregate collection of different economies operating around the world. Individual countries and the economies they adopt through regulation and policy-making tend to reflect one of three orientations: a command economy, a market economy, or a mixed economy (Albarran, 2002). In reality, all three types of economies are abstractions (much like theories), as are the labels used to represent them. Still, it offers a simple classification system that is helpful, especially in recognizing the role of the government to its respective media system. We will define each of these economies in more detail.

In a command economy the government regulates all aspects of economic activity; there is no such thing as an open or free market. The government controls all economic decision-making in regard to what goods to produce, how much it will produce, and what it will cost. Command economies have been in decline since the fall of the Berlin Wall in 1989, which was followed by the collapse of several Eastern European nations and the breakup of the former Soviet Union. However, two examples of command economies still exist: North Korea and Cuba.

Other countries such as Russia and China were formerly identified as command economies, but there have been many changes in both of these countries as they slowly progress towards more of a mixed economy. However, in terms of media ownership, command economies tend to own or control media very tightly. China and Russia have opened up portions of their economies to private or foreign investment and ownership, but the media systems in both of these countries remain under the strong control of the government. In China, the country's official press agent—Xinhua News—is a government-controlled entity. In this same sense North Korea and Cuba allow no private ownership of their media; all entities are state-controlled.

Another type of economy is the market economy, identified by a complex system of buyers and sellers, where prices and quantities produced are determined openly and freely through competitive market forces without any government involvement. In reality, there are no countries that operate in a truly open market economy without some type of government oversight or regulatory guidelines. Hence, of the three basic classifications, the market economy is idealized by those advocating a totally free market system without government intervention.

Most countries try to emulate the basic characteristics of the market economy through the establishment of a mixed economy. A mixed economy involves free market principles and ideals, but also features government regulation and oversight. The media systems in the United Kingdom and the United States are two of the largest examples of such systems in countries operating a mixed economy. In a mixed economy, the media is predominantly owned by private enterprises and perhaps even foreign investors as opposed to the government—but that doesn't mean the government has no ownership in the media. Many countries in Europe, Latin America, Asia, and Africa own national or regional broadcast channels (TV and radio) and also publish or subsidize some newspaper operations. For example, press subsidies are very common among the Scandinavian nations of Sweden, Finland, and Norway (e.g., Höyer, 1968; Picard & Gronlund, 2003). Many governments have remained at least partial owners of some media outlets in order to ensure the philosophy of pluralism, or serving the needs of the public rather than the marketplace.

The mixed economy often features government policies regarding both domestic and foreign ownership of media outlets, as well as other types of regulations over such areas as content and political advertising. A mixed economy is also apparent when advertising is one of the primary means of institutional support. Advertising is the way most media enterprises are subsidized in a mixed economy, as advertisers purchase time (broadcast) or space (press or Internet) in order to reach audiences drawn to media content. Yet another trait of a mixed economy is that of direct payments by consumers to media companies. For example, when purchasing a ticket to see a movie, a sound recording for your home or Mp3 player, or a subscription to cable television or a newspaper or magazine, you are sending payments to a private enterprise, which operates to make a profit. A mixed economy is usually identified with the philosophy of capitalism.

SUPPLY AND DEMAND

Supply and demand are two of the most important concepts in understanding economics and economic activity. Supply refers to the quantity of goods a producer will offer in a given market. Demand, on the other hand, represents the quantity of goods that buyers seek to acquire. Supply and demand function together in a market system, determining the price of the good or product as a result of the interplay of these two concepts.

Applied to the media industries, there are numerous examples of supply and demand at work. For example, in the motion picture industry, a movie studio will produce a certain number of films each year—the supply is limited by the money available for new productions as well as time to create a feature film. The demand by the audience for box office tickets also influences the production cycles—thus one reason we experience so many sequels year after year, such as franchises involving Harry Potter, the X-Men, and other characters. In print, newspapers and magazines base the amount of content they need to fill out their publications in conjunction with the demand for advertisers. As advertisers demand more space, it is easy to add pages; when demand declines, page counts can be reduced.

Radio and television stations can program only 24 hours a day, so in a sense there are constraints on the supply of programs they can offer at any given time. Likewise, TV and radio stations can program only so many minutes of commercial time (advertising) per hour; otherwise viewers and listeners may turn away.

A unique feature of the media industries is that their products can be reused over and over. TV programs, music, and movies can be recycled again and again, unlike barrels of oil or other commodities, which as consumed are gone. These media content products with long-term incremental value represent what Anderson (2006) calls the long tail. The long tail resembles a demand curve that follows a long downward trajectory (see Figure 3.1), suggesting that over time a popular movie, book, or sound recording will still be in demand long after it has obtained any sort of "hit" status, and it will be sought by smaller, niche buyers. The Internet, thanks to its ability to access servers

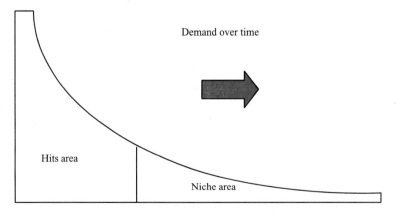

Figure 3.1 Graphical Description of the "Long Tail"

Source: Author rendition adapted from Anderson (2006).

with stored content, enhances long tail activity in regard to demand for media content.

PRICE

Price is the amount a good or service costs, determined as the result of supply and demand forces. Prices vary based on how the market is segmented. This is especially true across the media economy. We will examine this from the perspective of both advertisers and consumers.

In advertising, marketers pay for access to audiences via time and space in traditional media, and through subscriptions, click-through, and opt-in via websites and new media platforms. Advertisers know they will pay more for mediums that deliver larger audiences (such as television and newspapers) and less for mediums that deliver smaller audiences (radio). Likewise, advertisers will pay more for prime positions, such as in television evening hours when the largest audience is viewing, and in radio for morning drive time when audiences are commuting to work and school. With websites, audience activity is in the form of clicking through a set of options delivered from a search inquiry, selecting a banner advertisement, signing up for a subscription, or opting in (agreeing) to receive more information, which usually requires some sort of registration process. Marketers also know advertising will cost more to target high-income customers through vehicles like classical radio or publications like the *Economist* or the *Wall Street Journal*. Price levels vary across advertising, resulting in a form of segmentation depending on the type of vehicle and target audience desired.

Consumers are also sensitive to price, and while there is a tendency to classify consumers into three categories of household income (low, middle, and high) many levels of segmentation are possible. Price points become very sensitive to consumers at all levels of income, especially when economic conditions may decline. Consumer spending varies according to gender, life cycle, ethnicity, education, size of the household, and location (where people live). Some products are priced to target the higher end of the market (think in terms of luxury vehicles like a BMW or Mercedes) while others may appeal to the lower end of the spectrum (the Smart car).

As seen in these examples, the price of a product or service leads to segmentation of the market for both advertisers and consumers. In the media economy, prices are also impacted by what economists refer to as elasticity of demand, and the ability to substitute one product or service for another, known as cross-elasticity of demand.

PRICE ELASTICITY OF DEMAND

Price elasticity of demand helps us understand how prices vary in an economic system. The price for a good or product is the direct result of supply and demand functioning in a market, and because prices fluctuate and change price is considered elastic. Price elasticity of demand can be calculated by dividing the percentage change in quantity by the percentage change in price. If the formula is greater than 1.0, demand is considered elastic. If the result is 1.0, demand is considered unit-elastic. If the result is less than 1.0, demand is considered inelastic.

$$\text{Price elasticity of demand} = \frac{\text{Percentage change in quantity}}{\text{Percentage change in price}}$$

For example, in elastic demand, a change in price results in a proportionally greater change in the quantity demanded, which means revenues will increase. When personal computers were first introduced in the 1980s, prices were high. Over time, the price declined, leading to more households adopting their first computer. The decline in prices meant more sales of computers. In the media economy, elastic demand is typical for many types of consumer technologies, ranging across such items as laptops, HDTV receivers, DVD and Mp3 players, and mobile phones.

Unit-elastic demand occurs when there is a change in price, resulting in a proportionally equivalent change in demand. In other words, prices can either rise or fall, but the quantity demanded changes by proportionally the same amount. Thus revenues will remain unchanged.

Finally, inelastic demand occurs when a percentage change in quantity demanded is less than the percentage change in price. This means that, as prices decline, revenues will also decline. Generally speaking, goods and services for which there are no clear substitutes are considered inelastic.

It is important to recognize that price elasticity of demand is influenced by a number of exogenous variables such as household income, substitutability, necessity, and duration (e.g., the longer a price holds, the higher the elasticity). But a key trait of the media economy is that most products can be substituted for another, a concept known as cross-elasticity of demand.

CROSS-ELASTICITY OF DEMAND

While price elasticity assists in understanding demand, we must also recognize that there typically are comparable products and goods that can be substituted for one another. This concept is referred to as cross-elasticity of demand. In the media economy, cross-elasticity of demand is quite common.

For example, we drive to our local theater to see a new movie, only to learn the film we want to see is sold out for the rest of the evening. We could go home, or find another activity, but many people—since they are already at the theater—will simply buy tickets to see another film. The second movie may not have been our desired option, but it is an acceptable substitute. Likewise, when listening to your iPod or Mp3 player, you may want to hear a particular genre of music, so you focus on those selections rather than the other songs you have loaded on your player. Media products by their nature offer a great deal of substitutability, facilitating cross-elasticity of demand. There are so many media products—and so many different ways to consume these products—that it makes cross-elasticity a common practice.

Cross-elasticity of demand raises concerns for media companies and advertisers vying for our attention. Because there are so many choices for content available, this leads to increasing fragmentation of the audience into smaller and smaller sectors. As we add new digital platforms and other technologies to reach consumers, the problem is further magnified, giving consumers more control over when, where, and how to access media content.

OTHER FORMS OF DEMAND

In addition to price elasticity and cross-elasticity, there are other types of demand found in the media economy. The actual demand for the media content or product is one example. Normally, we think of this as taking place at the consumer level as we "consume" (watch, listen, or read) content products such as a movie, a television program, a sound recording, or a printed object. Consumers make decisions about content options based on their wants and needs, as well as the perceived utility and value derived from the content. These concepts will be introduced in the next section.

Another obvious type of demand comes from advertisers. Advertisers seek to have their messages seen and heard by audiences accessing the content; advertisers purchase time and space among media outlets to reach the audience. Advertisers for the most part are not concerned with the content, but they are very interested in the audience. Therefore

Table 3.1 Financial Support of Select Media Industries

INDUSTRY	PRIMARY REVENUES	SECONDARY REVENUES
Local broadcast TV	Local advertising	National advertising
Cable/satellite/IPTV operators	Subscriptions/fees	Advertising, equipment rentals
Radio	Local advertising	National advertising
Motion pictures	Box office sales	Home video, product placement
Music	Consumer purchases	License fees
Newspapers	Advertising (retail)	Subscriptions, per copy sales, classified advertising
Magazines	Advertising	Subscriptions, per copy sales
Books	Consumer purchases	License fees (movies, etc.)
Internet service providers	Subscriptions/fees	Advertising
Major websites	Consumer purchases	Advertising

Source: Author compilation.

Table 3.2 Key Media Mergers and Acquisitions, 1990–2008

YEAR	COMPANIES INVOLVED
1990	Time Inc. and Warner Communications Inc. ($14 billion)
1994	Viacom acquires Paramount ($10 billion) and Blockbuster ($8.4 billion)
1996	Walt Disney Company acquires Capital Cities/ABC ($19.6 billion)
1996	Time Warner acquires Turner Broadcasting System ($7.5 billion)
1999	Viacom acquires CBS, Inc. ($35.6 billion)
2000	Time Warner merges with America Online (AOL) ($165 billion)
2001	NBC acquires 80% ownership of Universal from Vivendi ($43 billion)
2004	NBC Universal acquires Telemundo ($1.98 billion, est.)
2006	Google acquires YouTube ($1.65 billion)
2007	News Corporation acquires Dow Jones Company ($5 billion)

Source: Compiled by the author from numerous sources. Year refers to the actual date the deal was completed. The values are reported from various news sites.

advertisers will seek to maximize exposure to their messages when they acquire time and space in the media economy. Advertising represents the primary form of revenues in most sectors of the media economy (see Table 3.1).

Yet another type of demand is the actual demand for media properties. Media properties include radio and television stations, newspapers, magazines, publishers, film studios, recording companies, and Internet service providers and search engines. Media mergers and acquisitions mushroomed in the 1980s and 1990s owing to a number of factors: low interest rates, plenty of available capital, and most importantly high demand for businesses with a history of strong profit margins. Table 3.2 lists a sample of some of the key media-related mergers and acquisitions from 1990 to 2008.

WANTS, NEEDS, UTILITY, AND VALUE

Wants, needs, utility, and value are four interrelated concepts functioning primarily at the consumer level that impact our individual demand for media content and media products. First, let's look at wants. A want is simply that: something that we as consumers desire. Wants enhance our life. They represent a wide variety of feelings. We may see a want as a pleasure or something that provides gratification. We may see a want as fulfilling a goal or a dream, or something to save us time and effort. Our wants are influenced by many things: our peers, family, institutions with which we interact (schools, churches, etc.) and especially culture and advertising.

Needs are more basic than wants. In the strictest sense, needs are things we need in order to survive, such as food, water, shelter, and clothing. We need a job or some sort of income in order to provide for our needs and those of others who depend on us. We also need some sense of structure or purpose in our lives. Needs are very basic, but, in a media-rich world filled with persuasive advertising messages, popular culture, and societies driven by consumption and acquisition, people often confuse wants with needs. Clearly, wants and needs drive a lot of consumer spending on all sorts of products and services, including media content products. Wants and needs are also influenced by utility and value.

Utility is best thought of as the satisfaction derived from using media products and services. For example, if you own an iPod Touch, you probably enjoy it for many reasons: portability, great audio and video quality, ease of operation, Internet access, and so on. In other words, your iPod Touch offers you a lot of utility when it comes to listening or watching media content. Your cell phone is another example. You originally acquired a cell phone so you could talk to friends and family; these old phones were limited in their utility. Today, we don't have just cell phones, but smart phones like the iPhone and BlackBerry. These phones offer a great deal of utility to consumers, with features like messaging, an Mp3/video player, GPS, a digital camera, a clock, a calculator, Internet access, and the ability to run all sorts of applications.

Economists define value as the worth or value we place on a particular product or service. Value is subjective in nature, because we value media products differently. For some, it might be a collection of DVDs or music. For others it might be video games or a particular book series. We assign value based on our own system of wants and needs.

Life stages also influence wants, needs, utility, and value, as do income, size of a household, and other demographic variables. For example, younger adults typically perceive more value and utility from a broad range of technology and media-related products, while older adults are often less enamored with technology and interested in more targeted products. As we grow and age, our wants and needs evolve, as do our perceptions of utility and value. This raises both opportunities and challenges for media enterprises, as these institutions try to develop content and products that will be interesting to consumers across many different lifestyles and demographic categories.

ALLOCATION

Allocation is a central part of economic decision-making; in the media economy allocation decisions are made by all parties. Suppliers must determine how many units of a product (e.g., a motion picture, a TV series, a book, etc.) to produce based upon available resources. Advertisers must make decisions about what messages to place in what mediums, depending on strategic goals and objectives as well as the amount of their budgets.

The individual level is where many allocation decisions are made. Consumers make allocation decisions related to media products and services based on their discretionary income as well as their time. In terms of expenditures, media spending continues to grow each year in developed countries like the United States (see Chapter 9 for a full discussion). But most individuals do not have unlimited financial resources, so they make decisions on how much money to spend on television (if they subscribe to cable, satellite, or IPTV), print material, Internet access, sound recordings, movie tickets and rentals, and so on. But, perhaps more importantly, individuals are constrained by time, as each of us has only 24 hours in a day and 168 hours in a week.

Each day consumers make numerous allocation decisions on how they spend their time and money, often out of habit or without a lot of discernment. Media companies know that the only way to entice and attract *new* consumers is through a combination of marketing (advertising, promotion, and other activities to increase awareness) and branding (e.g., logos, positioning statements, and slogans consumers will easily recognize). Each day, a "war" exists to gather out attention from numerous forms of advertising and promotion to brand names we see on clothing, accessories, and items we use on a daily basis. All of these efforts are designed to persuade consumers as they make allocation decisions. In a highly competitive, fragmented media environment, reaching consumers and attempting to influence their allocation decisions have become ever more challenging.

HORIZONTAL AND VERTICAL INTEGRATION

Horizontal and vertical integration represents a form of strategy employed by a media enterprise to determine how to create a competitive advantage in the marketplace. Both concepts are easy to understand, but such decisions on integration are usually made by larger firms and conglomerates. We'll begin with a discussion of horizontal integration.

Horizontal Integration

When a company decides to enter into different markets, it is engaging in horizontal integration. If a firm produced only one product or was active in only one market, this would represent a single-dimensional activity. This would be the case for a newspaper publisher that only publishes newspapers, but has no other holdings. This company's economic fate and fortune would be tied to the success of that single enterprise—the newspaper.

When companies expand into other related or non-related markets, they are engaging in horizontal integration—meaning they draw revenues (and losses) across business segments. Some segments may perform well, while others may not. A horizontal strategy is widely believed to help ride out fluctuations in the business cycle.

In this sense, horizontal integration is also thought of as a form of diversification. Several studies have examined diversification among media companies. Dimmick and Wallschlaeger (1986) studied diversification of TV network parent companies in relation to their activities into new media. Albarran and Porco (1990) examined diversification of firms involved in the premium cable market. Chan-Olmsted and Chang (2003) found a number of related products in the businesses of global media firms, while Kranenburg, Hagedoorn, and Pennings (2004) found that large publishing companies tended to diversify into related businesses.

A number of media companies engaged in horizontal diversification from 1980 to 2000 as media mergers and acquisitions were on the rise.

Several companies underwent profound change as their asset base changed owing to acquisitions. Before the Walt Disney Company acquired Capital Cities/ABC in the 1980s, its only media assets were the Disney Studios. Now Disney is one of the world's largest media companies. Time Warner started as a company publishing one magazine—*Time*. Now it is the largest media company in the world, with segments devoted to publishing, motion pictures, television, and music, to name just a few.

Vertical Integration

Vertical integration is identified as a firm's effort to control all aspects of creation, production, distribution, and exhibition, which form the media value chain. By being in control of all of these areas, the company could theoretically leverage their assets in the widest possible way, and engage in a number of cross-marketing and cross-promotional efforts in order to capture more revenues at the various stages of the value chain and, ideally, increase market share. Two examples of studies examining aspects of vertical integration are Chipty (2001) and Waterman (1993).

Vertical integration among media firms gained a great deal of attention in the 1980s with the merger of Time Inc. and Warner Communications to create Time Warner. The company significantly added to its asset base and vertical integration capabilities with the acquisition of the Turner Broadcasting System and all of its holdings (notably satellite channels CNN, Headline News, TNT, and Turner Classic Movies) in the early 1990s.

Time Warner had the ability: to create a motion picture through its ownership of Warner Brothers studio; to build awareness and interest in the movie through its printed magazines and other publications; to cross-promote the movie through other venues like feature stories on its satellite TV channels; to showcase the film via its ownership of premium channels Home Box Office and Cinemax (following the movie's box office run) and air it on the company's own cable TV systems; and finally to make it available to its TV syndication unit for both domestic and global distribution.

Time Warner's rush to vertical integration was mimicked to various degrees by other conglomerates, notably Viacom, Disney, and News Corporation. All of these companies followed the lead of Time Warner to create a vertically integrated conglomerate.

By the middle of the 2000s, many efforts were being trimmed back. Vertical integration still exists, but it is much tougher to implement and make work on a practical level. Viacom was the first conglomerate to deconsolidate, breaking itself into two separate companies—CBS and "new" Viacom, ending their vertical integration efforts. Disney sold some of their assets to focus more on core holdings like ESPN and its motion picture unit. Time Warner split off its cable television systems into a separate company in 2009.

Looking back, vertical integration was not a very successful strategy for media companies, and it was a very expensive strategy—costing billions of dollars over time. In the 21st century, the early trends have been to shed non-core assets that distract from the base of the company, and work on building strong brands and capturing market share for core holdings. At the same time, we see some new media companies— Google the best example—taking a different approach to vertical integration by attempting to be all things related to the Internet. Google is doing this by building on its success at search, but expanding with services like Gmail, Google Docs, Google Maps, Google Earth, and by the end of 2009 a new smart phone known as the Droid, designed to be a competitor to Apple's iPhone and Research in Motion's BlackBerry.

COMPETITION AND CONCENTRATION

Competition and concentration are two more interrelated concepts useful in understanding the functions of the media economy. Competition refers to the degree to which competitors compete for the same resources. Applied to the media economy, resources for which the media industries compete are audiences and advertisers. The media industries need both audiences and advertisers in order to grow their operations and survive.

Competition decisions among firms represent part of their strategic management efforts, described by Porter (1980) as a firm seeking a competitive advantage against other competitors. There is a strong body of literature related to media industry competition established by Dimmick (2003) and colleagues. Much of this work flows from application of the biological theory of the niche to the media economy, discussed in Chapter 2. With the advent of the Internet and multiple digital platforms, competition for audiences and advertisers has never been greater.

Competition is also of interest to policymakers and regulators, who want to ensure competitive markets in all sectors of the economy in order to stimulate the best pricing options for consumers. Competition is directly related to the concept of concentration. Concentration is a characteristic of a market's structure, exemplified by the theory of the firm presented in Chapter 2. Competition is non-existent in a monopoly, but grows as the number of competitors rise towards the oligopoly, monopolistic competition, and perfect competition sectors.

One of the biggest challenges for regulators is how to measure competition. Historically, when media-related markets were singular in nature and not intertwined, this was not difficult. In the 21st century, regulators are challenged by the dissolving of market boundaries and the degree of activity across markets. Measures of competition were established to assess the degree of concentration in a market. Common measures of concentration are usually tied to ratings, circulation, or revenues, and include the following tools and methodologies:

- *Concentration ratios.* These are typically used to measure the combined market shares of the top four or top eight firms in a market; they are also labeled as the CR4 or the CR8 (Albarran, 2002). If the combined shares of the top four firms equal or are greater than 50%, the market is considered concentrated. On the CR8, if the combined shares of the top eight firms equal or are greater than 75%, the market is considered concentrated.
- *The Lorenz curve.* This provides a graphical representation of competition by charting market shares on one axis in comparison to the number of firms on the other axis (Albarran, 2002). The departure from a 45° angle (which would resemble all firms capturing equal shares) is charted visually to show disparities among market share. The Lorenz curve is useful only with a limited number of firms, and provides limited utility.
- *Herfindahl-Hirschman index (HHI).* A more sophisticated measure to assess competition, the HHI is calculated by squaring the market shares of each firm and then determining if the degree of competition is high (>1,800), moderate (≥1,000 to ≤1,800), or unconcentrated (<1,000). The HHI is used by the U.S. Department of Justice Antitrust Division to assess the impact of concentration when reviewing mergers and acquisitions.

Noam (2009) provides the most detailed examination of media concentration to date, which should be of help to policymakers and scholars struggling with ways to address concentration in rapidly evolving markets. In detailing concentration of the media industries in the United States, Noam (pp. 432–433) develops a new model to assess concentration by introducing two new variables—lower barriers to entry and the growth of scale economies—and how they impact media industry concentration over time. Noam's work is impressive, and is a valuable addition to our understanding of concentration in the media.

SUMMARY

This chapter provides an overview of many of the key concepts used to understand the media economy. The chapter began with a discussion of the three types of economies found around the world (the command, market, and mixed economies), their philosophy and description.

Next, the chapter introduced the primary economic concepts of supply and demand, with particular relevance to and examples from the media economy. Closely related to supply and demand is price, examined from the perspectives both of the individual consumer and of the advertiser. From there the concepts of price elasticity of demand and cross-elasticity of demand were discussed. Demand was also discussed from other viewpoints, including the demand for media content, the demand for advertising, and the demand for media properties.

At the consumer level, the concepts of wants, needs, utility, and value were introduced, and their significance to understanding consumer behavior and how it is influenced in the media economy was pointed out. The concept of allocation was introduced next as a part of economic decision-making, with relevance to suppliers, advertisers, and individuals.

The chapter's introduction to key concepts concluded with a review of market variables, including horizontal and vertical integration, followed by a discussion of competition and concentration and how these two concepts are related. Tools used to measure concentration were reviewed, and their limitations in rapidly changing markets were discussed. A new model developed by Noam (2009), which holds promise on how to measure concentration in evolving markets, was briefly discussed.

The reader should recognize that this is not a complete discussion of all possible concepts related to the media economy. However, the chapter does provide a foundation as we move forward to an examination of the market in Chapter 4, followed by individual chapters focusing on the impact of technology, globalization, regulation, and social aspects and how they affect the media economy.

DISCUSSION QUESTIONS

1. Why is the mixed economy the dominant type of economy found around the world? If the mixed economy is so popular, why do we still have some nations operating with a command economy?

2. Price is a key economic concept in any society. How is price determined in the media economy? What are some of the factors media industries must consider when setting prices for information and entertainment products?

3. There are many different ways to examine demand in the media economy. Advertising is one of the most important. What role does advertising play in the media economy? How vital is advertising to the support of the media industries?

4. The chapter introduces the concepts of wants and needs. Are media-related products such as movies, sound recordings, TV programs, and magazines wants or needs? Why or why not?

5. How does horizontal and vertical integration relate to competition and concentration? What, if any, are the problems caused by increasing levels of media concentration?

CHAPTER 4

Evolving Markets in the Media Economy

In this chapter you will learn:

- how to define a market in the media economy;
- traditional approaches used to define media markets, including the theory of the firm;
- why media markets are constantly evolving across all levels of the media economy;
- the different forces impacting markets found in the media economy.

Building on the previous chapters regarding economic theories and concepts used in understanding the media economy, this chapter focuses on the market itself and how markets are evolving across the media economy in the 21st century. The classical definition of a "market" in economic terms refers to the location where suppliers and buyers meet to determine the price of goods. Picture this type of activity held centuries ago, when merchants and farmers would bring their goods for sale to a town market and would engage in negotiations with potential buyers wanting their goods.

Today this type of market activity still exists through venues like the stock, commodity, and financial exchanges on Wall Street and other economic centers around the globe, but there are also countless market activities occurring in many different locations, at many different times and places across business and industry. The market in the media economy is the aggregate of many supply and demand situations involving advertising, content, technology, and other media-related firms. In the media economy, market activity takes place business to business, between consumers and business, and even from consumers to

Table 4.1   Examples of Market Activity in the Media Economy

TYPE OF MARKET	EXAMPLES OF MARKET ACTIVITY
Business to business (B2B)	Advertising in both traditional and online media, mergers and acquisitions, direct investment, credit, partnerships, joint ventures.
Business to consumer (B2C)	Purchase of books, sound recordings, magazines, newspapers, movie tickets, digital content (subscriptions, single copies, pay per use); any area that involves direct consumer purchases from a media business.
Consumer to consumer (C2C)	Auction sites like eBay, Amazon consumer storefronts, Craigslist, social networks.

Source: Author compilation.

consumers (see Table 4.1). Transactions and market acquisitions can occur in physical settings or via cyberspace with Internet-based transactions (e-commerce).

DEFINING THE MEDIA MARKET

Traditionally, the field of media economics has defined a media market as consisting of a product dimension and a geographical dimension (Picard, 1989). The product is the newspaper, motion picture, sound recording, television program, podcast, or any other media-related product. The geographical dimension reflects where the products are offered, which can range from a local media product (e.g., a newspaper or broadcast of a radio or TV station) to the global market for media products (e.g., movies, television programs, and sound recordings).

According to Picard (1989), a unique aspect of the media industries is the ability to offer the product in two separate but related markets: the market for audiences and the market for advertisers. This is referred to as the "dual" product market. Not every industry is engaged in the sale of advertising, but most media products are advertiser-supported (see Table 4.2). Yet another unique trait of the media economy is the ability to reuse media products over and over, and to sell them to different audiences and different advertisers. This repurposing of media products has been enhanced by the development of digitally based content, which has made products more accessible but also more prone to piracy and theft.

Table 4.2 Examples of Advertiser-Supported Media Products

MEDIUM	PRODUCTS
Electronic media	Broadcast radio and television stations and networks; syndicated programs; cable-, satellite-, and IPTV-delivered channels.
Print	Newspapers (daily, weekly); magazines.
Motion pictures	Product placement; merchandise tie-ins.
Internet	Search engines; banner advertising; click-through advertising; Internet TV; Internet service providers (portals).
New media/digital platforms	Online TV; podcasts; blogs; smart phones; social networks; user-generated content.

Source: Author compilation.

TRADITIONAL APPROACHES TO DEFINING THE MARKET

While economists, financial analysts, scholars, and students have an interest in defining media markets, regulators and policymakers also play an important role in how markets are defined, as they want to promote competition and limit anti-competitive behaviors. This is typically a public policy goal in those countries functioning with a mixed economy. By establishing guidelines, regulators seek to maximize a competitive market system whereby consumers benefit (i.e., favorable social policy) and concentration is limited.

Historically, media markets have been defined by analyzing the specific product and geographical dimensions, assessing trends and patterns, and determining the extent of market competition and concentration. Such an analysis also enabled the field to identify media markets according to their market structure—a theorized construct defining market activity primarily along a continuum ranging from a monopoly to perfect competition, sometimes referred to as "the theory of the firm" (Gomery, 1989). Let's briefly define these labels for markets:

- *Monopoly.* A monopoly occurs when there is only one seller of a product. It is assumed there is no close substitute for the product. The monopolist sets the price in the market since there are no competitors.
- *Duopoly.* A duopoly simply means there are two competitors in the market space, and the firms split the market. Pricing is relatively similar and is set by the firms. Duopoly firms are very

interdependent, meaning the actions of one firm impact the other firm.

- *Oligopoly.* An oligopoly consists of a small number of sellers that dominate the market, typically between three and ten competitors. Products tend to be homogeneous, and pricing is set by the leader and other firms follow suit, but usually there are not huge variances in pricing. In an oligopoly, firms are considered interdependent or related to one another in terms of business practices and market behavior, as each firm controls a defined share of the market, and each firm wants to hold on to its share.
- *Monopolistic competition.* In this type of structure there are many sellers or suppliers of products that are similar but not ideal substitutes for one another. In a monopolistic competition structure, the firms engage in product differentiation to slightly distinguish their products from one another. Because of stronger competition in this type of structure, price is set by a combination of market forces and the firms themselves.
- *Perfect competition.* Here there are numerous suppliers offering the same product, one of which is easily substituted for another. No single seller has influence over another; therefore the market sets the price.

Figure 4.1 illustrates how the primary media industries would be aligned along a continuum of market structure labels. The problem with this approach is that the media industries are constantly redefining themselves, making it challenging to categorize a media industry into a definitive market structure. Monopolistic markets have all but vanished owing to a combination of technological, regulatory, and globalization forces (all discussed in more detail in later chapters). With the exception of websites, there are no examples of perfect competition across the media economy.

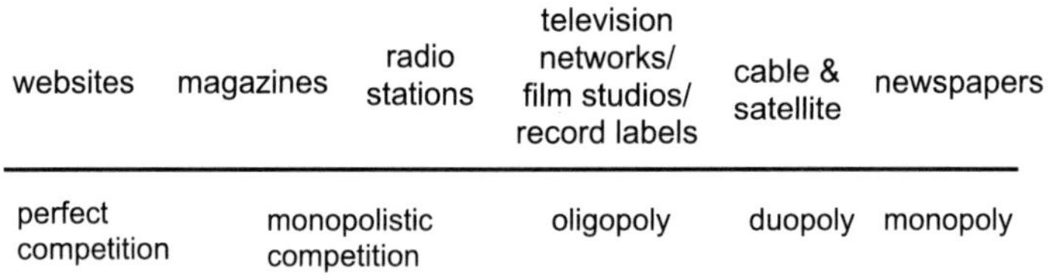

websites	magazines	radio stations	television networks/ film studios/ record labels	cable & satellite	newspapers
perfect competition		monopolistic competition	oligopoly	duopoly	monopoly

Figure 4.1 Media Industries Representing Traditional Market Structure

Source: Author's compilation.

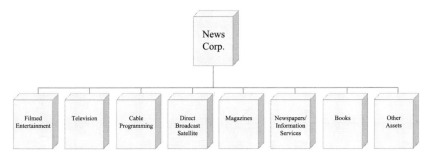

Figure 4.2 News Corporation Market Segments (2009)

Source: http://www.newscorp.com/ (retrieved September 30, 2009).

Another challenge with this approach to market structure is that the focus is only on the internal market, or what is referred to as within-industry activity (Albarran & Dimmick, 1996). If we apply a strict definition, such as English-language broadcast network TV in the U.S., this market consists of only a few firms: ABC, CBS, NBC, Fox, CW, and MyTV. This approach would be fine if these firms participated only in the single broadcast network television market, but we know they are engaged in distributing content many other ways than just broadcast. In fact, most media firms seek to maximize their market share horizontally, or across industries.

Media companies now participate in several markets simultaneously. For example, News Corporation is one of the largest media companies in the world, led by Rupert Murdoch, its chief executive officer. Figure 4.2 depicts the major segments or markets in which News Corporation is engaged. And, within these individual markets, the company is engaged in a number of other sub-markets.

In the television segment (illustrated in Figure 4.3), the company lists ownership of two TV networks (Fox Broadcasting Company and MyNetwork TV), a group of TV stations, Fox Sports Australia, and STAR, a set of global television channels. Within these specific entities there are various digital platforms offering content via the Internet, mobile phones, podcasts, and social networks, meaning there are many sub-markets where Fox as a company is competing for market share. Clearly, the "television" segment for News Corporation is much more than just television. How can we define the specific market the company is engaged in when in fact News Corporation is engaged in multiple markets? Further, how could regulators begin to define the market?

Labeling markets using the terms of monopoly, oligopoly, monopolistic competition, and perfect competition served the field of

Figure 4.3 News Corporation Television Segment (2009)

Source: http://www.newscorp.com/operations/television.html (retrieved September 30, 2009).

media economics well for its first 50 years of inquiry (circa 1948–1998), but these terms now have limited utility. In today's media economy these areas of market activity are not reflective of the full range of market activities by media firms, especially those that own a portfolio of media-related brands and products. What is needed is a new way to define media markets.

EVOLVING MARKETS IN THE MEDIA ECONOMY

In reality, what has happened is that many media markets have evolved to represent a more common structure, especially in those countries where the media industries have become concentrated. A hybrid type of market structure now exists, combining elements of an oligopoly market with a monopolistic competitive structure. In this type of structure, there are the leading firms that usually control as much as 80% of the market, and a group of smaller firms fighting for the remaining share. We find this structure present in markets like motion pictures, sound recordings, network television, and cable television to mention a few.

Albarran and Dimmick (1996) were among the first to recognize this evolving structure. A follow-up study (Albarran, 2003) used

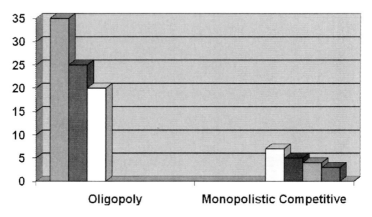

Figure 4.4   Hybrid Market Structure

Source: Author's rendition. In this example, the top three firms forming the oligopoly side of the hybrid market control about 80% of the market. All of the other firms, symbolized by the four smaller columns, compete for the remaining 20% share of the market in the monopolistic competition segment of the market.

concentration ratios and found that most media markets in the U.S. were highly concentrated, and the media and communications sector as a whole was very concentrated. Sheth and Sisodia (2002) also describe this same type of structure in their analysis of markets and industries using what the authors describe as "the rule of three." The rule of three posits that, in any industry, there are three leaders who dominate market share, and the remaining firms compete for the remainder. In essence, Sheth and Sisodia (2002) describe a hybrid structure as depicted in Figure 4.4.

Still another way to look at media markets would be to identify them by their core function rather than by focusing on the name of the medium. For decades, media economists have described a media value chain (see Figure 4.5) that could serve as a starting point for such an analysis. The terms content and distribution are particularly relevant.

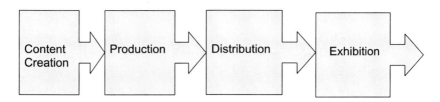

Figure 4.5   Traditional Media Value Chain

Source: Author's rendition.

For example, content can be broken down as needed into specific areas such as film and television content, audio (music) content, publishing, and user-generated content. Likewise, distribution can be broken down, considering such areas as broadcasting (networks, stations), multichannel television (cable, satellite, IPTV), or web distribution (services such as Hulu.com, TV.com, etc.).

We have seen new markets emerge that intersect with the media industries that may not necessarily involve core functions like content creation or distribution but are nevertheless important in understanding how markets have evolved and are interrelated. Here are a few examples of these new markets whose functions intersect with the activities of many media companies:

- *Search*. This represents the primary activity that takes place when a person connects to the Internet. Users go to the Internet for a variety of motivations, but we know that seeking information is one of the primary uses. An entire industry has developed around "search," led by market leaders Google, Yahoo!, and Microsoft's Bing. Most of the advertising spent online is invested in the "search" arena. These search functions often intersect with media companies and media content, identifying potential links to images, video, and audio files.
- *Social networking*. Social networking is another area where market lines are blurred. Social media websites like Facebook, MySpace (owned by News Corporation), LinkedIn, and Twitter have been phenomenally successful, and allow the user to share information with their own network of contacts and friends and to expand their network through access to their friends' networks. While business and industry were initially slow to recognize the potential of social networking, it is now a critical strategic component for every type of business enterprise (see Li & Bernoff, 2008; Shirky, 2008). Of course, many media companies already have a presence across numerous social networks, aimed at connecting users, building brands, and collecting feedback on their products and services.
- *User-generated content*. Websites like YouTube, Wikipedia, Craigslist, Flickr, and literally thousands of blogs allow users to share content with their friends and social networks, regardless of whether they created the content or it was created by another source. The media industries initially fought against services like YouTube, arguing the service infringed on their copyrights by

using programs without the owner's permission. By 2009, many media companies had reached settlements with the company. Recognizing YouTube's unique success (see Burgess & Green, 2009), many media companies negotiated rights for access to their content, realizing the site offered opportunities to reach new audience members and extend their reach.

Wikipedia and other "wiki" sites allow for audience members not only to create new content in the form of online encyclopedia entries, but also to edit and enhance existing entries (Tapscott & Williams, 2008). Wikis promote collaboration among users and, while users can post inaccurate or even bogus information, wikis will continue to grow in terms of popularity and utility.

New markets have also emerged related to technology in the form of hardware which serves as both a reception technology and a content playback device. Here are a few of the more promising hardware markets that now vie for the time and attention of audiences and consumers:

- *Smart phones.* Smart phones will continue to emerge as an important market, because these devices are really handheld computers that provide connectivity for mobile users. Apple's iPhone and Research in Motion's BlackBerry models integrate many tools for the user: Internet access, email, messaging, Mp3 player, video player, camera, calendar, note pad, games, hundreds of applications for every topic imaginable, and their core function—the ability to make and receive telephone calls. Today every media company has a mobile strategy, and recognizes this is another evolving market in which firms must be active in order to engage audiences.
- *Video game consoles.* Video game consoles, which initially only played games, have evolved into devices that blend different functions, such as content and distribution. The market is dominated by three players (Sony, Nintendo, and Microsoft), and the consoles are constantly being redesigned to offer new features and options for users. For example, the Sony PlayStation is equipped with a Blu-ray DVD player, which was a key factor in defeating Toshiba's rival HD-DVD, as the game console provided added utility as a playback device for movies and other content. The PlayStation also allows users to play audio CDs, and can connect to the Internet for online gaming. Video game

consoles will continue to add features as new models are introduced, giving media companies another path to consumers.

OTHER FORCES IMPACTING MARKETS

While markets are transforming across the media economy, it is not just internal forces that are causing markets to evolve. Markets also are continually impacted by external forces. Among these forces are economic conditions, technology, globalization, regulation, social aspects, access to capital, and the labor market. While these topics were briefly introduced in the first chapter, here we focus on how these forces impact markets across the media economy. Several of these forces will be expanded on later in individual chapters, providing more context and detail.

Economic Conditions

Economic conditions refer to the environment in which the markets are operating at any given time. Typically, economies move throughout various stages identified as recession, expansion, and stability. In a recession, economic activity curtails, and can range from a minor or short-term recession lasting just a few months to a longer-term situation resembling depression-like characteristics (unemployment in excess of 30%, significant reduction in GDP, high inflation, etc.). Recessions can occur for many reasons. In the United States, the recession that hit in 1929 was the result of instability in the financial markets, resulting in a huge loss for the stock market and many businesses and banks failing. In 2007 the U.S. would enter into the second-worst economic recession in history as the stock market lost nearly 60% of its value, also owing to problems in the financial sector. In Mexico and many Latin American countries, recessions have been caused by the devaluation of the local currency by the local governments in an effort to prevent runaway inflation and a total economic collapse. Japan, which represents one of the world's largest GDPs, came close to a financial collapse during the early 1990s.

A recession is particularly hard for markets operating in the media economy. Job losses usually happen first, causing people without work to restrict their discretionary spending. This in turn impacts businesses, as their sales suffer. Advertising typically contracts in a downward economic cycle, as businesses try to cut expenses and boost revenues. As advertising declines, this results in many media enterprises being forced to cut costs. This will lead media companies to eliminate jobs as well. Markets also experience declines in capital expenditures (discussed in Chapter 10) and other expenses, resulting in slower economic activity and furthering a recessionary environment. A severe recession means consumers may cut discretionary spending involving media products (e.g., subscriptions to cable or satellite, direct purchases, rentals).

History tells us that the downward cycle will at some point hit bottom and eventually begin an upward movement as the economy starts to grow once again. As the movement picks up momentum and accelerates, this part of the cycle is referred to as an expansion of an economy. In an expansion everything seems to move perfectly in sync; capital is flush; companies are investing in equipment, technology, and personnel; jobs are plentiful; competition is strong; interest rates are usually low; and economic indicators such as GDP show growth and potential for further expansion along with robust financial market activity.

Expansion in the media economy can be realized in several different ways. Firms can expand, either through mergers or acquisitions or via internal investment in research and development and production of new products and services. Advertising, the primary source of revenues, grows and is able to capture higher prices in negotiations for time and space. Innovation is widespread, and consumers spend money on new technologies, content products, digital platforms, and electronic commerce. An expansion varies in terms of size and time, meaning there is no exact percentage of growth to signal an expansion, nor is there an average time as to how long an expansion will last. When an expansion follows a recession, it may or may not recapture all of the value and GDP lost in the previous recession.

There are periods of time in the economic cycle when the markets are neither expanding nor declining; this is referred to as stability. In a stable market, "average" market activity takes over, thus replacing what can seem like a frenetic cycle during an expansion. Markets are the first to recognize when stability begins to happen, as revenues typically peak, investment activity slows, and other indicators begin to flatten. Stability can occur when markets are moving in a slow expansion, or even towards a slow decline, without going into a full recession.

Media markets in a stable environment experience advertising inventory and prices for advertising keeping pace with moderate growth, but not as quickly as in a full expansion. Merger and acquisition activity is present, but often slows down. Employment usually peaks as well. New content products and services may be withheld from the market, preferring to wait until the business cycle is more favorable towards long-term growth.

Technology

Technology is one of the most disruptive forces in the media economy, primarily because media markets are technologically dependent from all positions on the traditional media value chain: production, distribution, and exhibition. Media firms demand the latest technology, and are constantly updating both their physical hardware and the software needed to keep pace. Consumers are technologically oriented, with younger demographic segments among the savviest users, who require the latest tools and toys in the form of smart phones, Mp3 players, netbook computers, and other devices.

Technology offers positive and negative consequences. During the second half of the 20th century, technology alone resulted in the loss of many jobs as media companies transitioned from an analog to a digital environment. Everything from robotic cameras in television studios to word processing in newspaper publishing resulted in the loss of personnel and changing skill sets for many jobs. It used to take three people to shoot a television news story: the reporter, a camera operator, and a person to handle lighting and help if needed with audio. Now, all of this is done by one person working in the field with nothing more than a small video camera, and a mobile phone or a laptop to distribute the story back to their virtual newsroom. So, while technology has eliminated many jobs, it has also raised the bar for employees with multiple technical skills, and the ability to multitask in moving from different applications and also able to write, shoot, edit, and produce content.

Technology can be expensive to maintain and to replace, but while this represents expenditures for media firms it also creates opportunities for manufacturers, suppliers, and innovators of new technology to sell their products and services. As the media are technologically intensive industries, sweeping changes such as the transition to digital television, the introduction of smart phones, and the development of high-definition television spur interest, awareness, and ultimately greater use and consumption among consumers. More discussion of technology and its impact on the media economy is presented in Chapters 5 and 6.

Globalization

Globalization has many terms, but here we will think of it as a way companies reach beyond their domestic borders to engage consumers in other nations, thus expanding their markets (Friedman, 2005). Globalization directly impacts media markets in that more competitors enter the market. In the media sector, globalization has traditionally revolved around selling content, a practice that first began with Hollywood films and later television programming. The United States is the largest exporter of media content in the world, raising many concerns about American influence abroad and the notion of "cultural imperialism" (Jayakar & Waterman, 2000).

Globalization also occurs when companies acquire other properties in other countries. News Corporation was first an Australian newspaper company, acquiring newspapers in the United Kingdom and the United States, and later purchasing a group of television stations that would eventually become the Fox TV Network. Sony entered the film industry by first acquiring Columbia Tristar and later MGM.

Yet another form of globalization occurs when a company establishes multiple locations in other nations. The Nielsen Company, a privately held firm specializing in various types of audience research services, operates in over 100 countries throughout the world. Disney operates theme parks in several global cities, with a separate base in Latin America. The global leader in book publishing, Bertelsmann, also has operations around the world through its various publishing entities. Globalization is discussed in more detail in Chapter 7.

Regulation

Regulation is a central aspect of any government, establishing law and policy as needed to regulate markets and positively influence economic activity. Regulation takes place at various levels across the media economy, meaning policy initiatives can be: global in nature (such as with the World Trade Organization and the International Monetary Fund); regional, involving different countries (exhibited by the creation of trade blocs like the European Union, the North American Free Trade Agreement [NAFTA], and Asia-Pacific Economic Cooperation [APEC]); national, via a government's own laws and policies; at the state and local levels, where applicable through various agencies, councils, commissions, and other regulatory bodies (see, for example, King & King, 2009).

Any general regulatory action that impacts business activities (e.g., taxation, labor laws, interest rates, monetary policy) also affects media markets. However, there is a combination of regulatory activity that takes place among the typical executive–legislative–judicial branches of a government that function in tandem with a number of agencies that operate at the nation-state or local levels, and all influence media markets.

Using the United States as an example, the executive branch

represented by the President and Cabinet appoint individuals to agencies such as the Federal Communications Commission (FCC) and the Federal Trade Commission (FTC) with the advice and consent of the Senate. The legislative branch, through Congress, can propose new laws and regulations that can alter media markets, such as the sweeping 1996 Telecommunications Act, which liberalized ownership requirements and eased barriers to media industries competing with one another. The judicial branch is tied to the various court systems in the country, and interprets laws and challenges to laws assessing their constitutionality, especially those that may someway impose restrictions guaranteed by the First Amendment of the U.S. Constitution.

In addition to the regulatory activities of the three branches of government and a host of other agencies, there are other influences on the regulatory process. In any democracy, regulation is directly influenced by the people, who vote for their leaders and government representatives. Citizen groups and watchdog agencies have a history of influencing regulation of media markets. Critics play another role of influence in the regulatory process. Finally, the media industries themselves engage in their own form of self-regulation by enacting guidelines to attempt to limit government intrusion with new regulation or policy efforts. A closer look at regulation as a force impacting the media economy is presented in Chapter 8.

Social Aspects

Social aspects refer to the consumers and audiences that use the actual media products. Social aspects have taken on a much more important role in the 21st century, as the audience can no longer be thought of as a mass entity, but an aggregate of many different demographic, ethnic, and lifestyle groups with different needs and interests (Parrillo, 2009). The audience is constantly transforming (Napoli, 2003). The baby boomer generation is graying; American society along with many other nations is becoming much more ethnically diverse and multicultural; people are living longer and working longer; younger people are more technologically savvy and prefer to access content differently than adults.

Given all the outlets available for entertainment and information in a digitally delivered media world, audience fragmentation is at an all-time high. Audience members are more empowered than at any other time in media history. Audience members no longer just consume content—they also make content in a multitude of ways, whether through blogging, podcasting, uploading videos, or social networking, to name just a few options. Social aspects are yet another force driving the transformation process. More on social aspects is offered in Chapter 9.

Access to Capital

Money or capital is a key driver in any business or industry, and companies must have access to capital in order to conduct business. The economic crisis of 2007–2009 clearly demonstrated the vital role capital and credit play in the business world. We could easily observe the consequences as economies fell into severe recessions and capital became restricted, choking off money needed for business to meet payroll, acquire capital investments, and other needs. A global financial crisis was averted only by the G-20 nations taking unprecedented steps during the fall of 2008 into the spring of 2009 to flood their respective markets with working capital to encourage more credit loans and spur economic activity.

In terms of the impact on media markets, without capital new productions (whether movies or TV programs or new "albums") were put on hold; advertisers greatly reduced buying time, which in turn forced media companies to engage in massive expense cuts and job layoffs; promotion and marketing budgets were slashed; and virtually no mergers or acquisitions were even discussed.

Access to working capital is a must for any industry, especially those operating in the media economy. Chapter 10 takes an expanded look at this subject, along with a discussion of valuation and investment.

Labor

Labor is the backbone of any business enterprise, and the media economy requires workers who are able to multitask, make quick decisions under time pressures, and carry many different sets of job skills. The labor segment of the media economy is constantly changing, owing to many of the forces already discussed in this section—with technology being the main driver.

The media economy remains a strong area for various craft guilds and unions that wield their power and influence to negotiate wage scales and other concessions to benefit their members. While unions and guilds are not present in all parts of the world, they are very evident in countries with production of high-quality media products (e.g., the United Kingdom, the United States, Germany, France, Spain, etc.). Education also influences the labor market through preparation for careers and continuing learning opportunities.

Labor is a two-sided sword for management in that labor is needed to help a media enterprise achieve its goals and objectives, but at the same time labor is the most expensive area of any business. An expanded view of labor in the media economy is presented in Chapter 11.

SUMMARY

This chapter has discussed the role of the market in the media economy, beginning with how markets are defined in regard to economic activity. Markets in the media economy represent an aggregate of many supply and demand situations involving such areas as advertising, content, technology, and other media firms. Market activity occurs between businesses, between consumers and businesses, and between consumers and other consumers.

Media markets have been traditionally defined as dual-product markets because the product or good is usually made available to two distinct markets: advertisers and consumers. Media markets have also been defined by their geographical location. These product and geographical dimensions have been used for decades by policymakers, scholars, and students to understand market behavior. Labels of traditional types of market structure (e.g., monopoly, duopoly, oligopoly, monopolistic competition, perfect competition) were used from economics to classify media markets.

However, these approaches have limited utility in the 21st century owing to the transformation and evolution of markets in the media economy because, in reality, market activity occurs simultaneously across multiple levels and can be observed both within and across media industries. The chapter argues that a hybrid structure of media markets now exists across most areas of the media economy, represented by a small set of firms resembling an oligopoly that controls 70–90% of a market, with a number of smaller firms resembling a monopolistic competition structure fighting for the remaining 10–30% share.

The chapter also argues for markets to be defined using their core functions such as content and distribution to provide additional analysis. Suggestions for other functions and classifications were offered in the chapter, including search, social networking, user-generated content, smart phones, and video game consoles.

The chapter concluded with a discussion on external forces impacting markets in the media economy, including economic conditions, technology, globalization, regulation, social aspects, access to capital, and the labor market. Media markets, like markets in other areas of business activity, will continue to evolve and transform.

Students, scholars, media professionals, and policymakers all have a vested role in following the evolution and transformation of media markets, to fully understand how markets function in the media economy.

DISCUSSION QUESTIONS

1. Why are media-related markets more challenging to define in the 21st century?
2. How useful are the traditional labels of monopoly, oligopoly, monopolistic competition, and perfect competition in analyzing media markets in the 21st century? How can our definition of market structure be improved?
3. The chapter points out that in many segments of the media economy a hybrid structure exists. What are the two components that make up this hybrid structure?
4. Economic conditions, technology, globalization, regulation, social aspects, access to capital, and the labor market all impact markets. Briefly explain how each of these forces impacts media markets.

CHAPTER 5

Multi-Platform Media Enterprises

In this chapter you will learn:

- why media firms must be thought of as enterprises delivering content to multiple platforms in the media economy;
- many of the platforms media firms are using to attract audiences and advertisers;
- how consumers have evolved as multi-platform users;
- strategies and business models used by multi-platform media enterprises;
- case studies detailing how four different media companies are using multi-platform distribution across the media economy.

In the 21st century, media companies with roots in "old" or traditional media continue to evolve into multi-platform media enterprises. For decades, media content was delivered to one platform—newspapers, TV and radio broadcasts, and magazines. The adoption of digital technology enabled content to be shared among many different platforms. Media companies now distribute content to multiple platforms and devices. The term "enterprise" is used to illustrate the concept that media companies are no longer limited to a single distribution platform but rather operate as entities with the ability to offer content on many different platforms simultaneously.

The shift towards media companies becoming multi-platform enterprises was driven by technology, discussed more fully as a force impacting the media economy in Chapter 6. Multi-platform media enterprises can choose from a wide variety of content distribution platforms, including the traditional platforms as well as many new distribution options. A television station as a multi-platform media enterprise broadcasts its programs over the air, makes them available on the Internet, via mobile phones, and through video on demand, and offers additional content through social media sites like Facebook and Twitter. A radio station as a multi-platform media enterprise broadcasts programming on AM, FM, or HD channels, and also streams content on the Internet, offers a variety of podcasts, and uses social networking pages to share information, gather research, and build audiences. A book publisher as a multi-platform media enterprise prints titles in hard and soft covers, and also makes manuscripts available as audio books, online downloads for electronic book readers, and podcast versions.

This chapter begins with a discussion of the main distribution platforms used by media enterprises to deliver content. Other sections examine the consumer as a multi-platform user, and strategies and business models used in delivering content via multiple platforms. The chapter concludes with a series of short case studies illustrating multi-platform efforts involving a variety of media enterprises.

PRIMARY DISTRIBUTION PLATFORMS

This section examines the many distribution platforms available for media companies to reach consumers as of late 2009. Of course, not all of these platforms are available in every country, so this list reflects those available in the U.S., but many other nations will have these platforms in some version or another soon. Table 5.1 provides a list of these platforms.

As seen in Table 5.1, there are many paths available to deliver video and audio entertainment and information, from the standpoint both of distribution options and of reception technologies. Let's examine some of these distribution platforms in a bit more detail:

Table 5.1 Multiple Platforms to Reach Consumers

High-definition TV (HDTV)	Wi-Fi/WiMAX	Satellite radio
Multicast TV	Video game consoles	Internet radio
Video on demand (VOD)	Mobile/smart phones	HD radio
Internet TV	Blogs	Mp3 players
Broadband	Social media	Podcasts/videocasts
Digital video recorders	User-generated content	Personal digital assistants
DVD/Blu-ray	SMS/MMS	iPod Touch/iPad
Slingbox/Apple TV	RSS feeds	e-Book readers

Source: Compiled by the author from various sources.

- The Internet has become the primary content distribution platform for media companies. Whether it is Internet TV or radio, social media, or podcasts and videocasts, the Internet is the backbone for delivering most content. Users have a variety of ways to connect to the Internet, ranging from desktop, laptop, and netbook computers to handheld devices like mobile phones, Mp3 players, or PDAs. When the Internet emerged as a mass medium in the 1990s, traditional media companies as well as Internet-only companies began building their online presence in order to reach audiences via the web. For example, Hulu.com has become a major online distribution platform for the broadcast networks in the U.S. This is also known as webcasting, which in its broadest sense means distributing various forms of content (texts, images, audio, and video) via the Internet (Ha & Ganahl, 2007).
- Video on demand (VOD) is offered by cable, satellite, and IPTV providers to deliver movies and other programs to subscribers. VOD allows good functionality in that the user can pause, rewind, or fast-forward content. VOD is offered as part of a subscription package or on a per-view basis.
- Mobile platforms deliver content to smart phones and other handheld devices (Mp3 players, iPod Touch, etc.) using applications users can download for free or for a small fee. Mobile video is expected to grow exponentially over the next decade; one study estimated that mobile video revenues could reach over $3 billion by 2012 in the United States alone (*BIA's the Kelsey Group forecasts*, 2009).
- Social media sites were at first ignored by many media companies, but the rapid growth of Facebook, MySpace, Twitter, and especially YouTube forced media companies to recognize the need to have a social media strategy. YouTube has numerous channels with ties to traditional broadcast television, and services like Facebook, MySpace, and Twitter offer new ways to interact with audiences.

There are other distribution platforms available to reach audiences, as listed in Table 5.1. The good news for media companies is that there are more platforms than ever to reach audiences. The bad news for media companies is the costs to develop, maintain, and update so many platforms, along with the added challenge of trying to monetize revenues from these platforms.

CONSUMERS AS MULTI-PLATFORM USERS

With more media companies distributing content to multiple platforms, a key question arises as to how multi-platform distribution impacts the way that audiences consume various types of content available via different platforms and devices. Contemporary audiences are cross-platform consumers; they access and consume content via a wide variety of platforms and devices. These audiences, especially younger audiences, are also adept at multitasking, meaning they will surf the Internet while watching TV or listening to music. Let's examine what we know about how users are viewing online television through the Internet.

Online TV Viewing

As mentioned earlier, traditional media companies like television networks were hesitant to offer content on other platforms, fearing it would further fragment the audience from watching the program. However, the opposite is true—the chances of capturing a larger audience over time are greater by making the content available to multiple consumer platforms. This aggregate viewing (in the case of television) is larger than the number that will watch the regular broadcast.

There are numerous studies conducted about online TV viewing, what people are watching, and where they are watching. Here is a small sample of interesting findings:

- According to the Conference Board, one out of four households watches online television, up from 20% in 2008 (*TV viewing moves online*, 2009).
- Nine out of ten viewers watch online TV from home; one out of ten watches from work (*TV viewing moves online*, 2009).
- An earlier study by ABI Research found online viewing doubled from 2007 to 2008, with nearly 53% of viewers under age 29 watching at least once a month (Reardon, 2008).
- A 2008 study conducted by Nielsen and the Cable Television Association for Marketing found that one-third of all respondents watched some television programs online (Murph, 2008).

Clearly, online TV viewing is growing, especially with younger audiences. While many audiences prefer to watch TV on their regular or large-screen sets, online viewing has become more popular. Long-term, could the growth of online TV viewing influence some consumers to eliminate subscriptions to cable TV or satellite services?

Behind the popularity of online TV viewing is the basic idea of control. Consumers have control over what content they want to consume, at the time most convenient to them. Online TV viewing represents a huge change for traditional media companies, which used to control consumption through distribution over a single platform— the TV channel, newspaper, or radio station. Now that power has shifted to the consumer.

As consumers continue to adopt and access multiple platforms, they take more control of their consumption of media content. While it is great for the consumer, it is a challenge for media companies as the audience fragments into smaller and smaller segments with so many options available. Further, advertisers have had to rethink how to deliver messages in this fragmented, time-shifting, multi-platform environment.

STRATEGIES AND BUSINESS MODELS OF MULTI-PLATFORM MEDIA ENTERPRISES

Changing audience behaviors have forced media companies to distribute content across different platforms. In rethinking media companies as multiple-platform media enterprises, media firms must understand their audiences' needs and wants in order to deliver a better experience for consumers (Nielsen Company, 2009). Media enterprises also want to maximize the profits that can be generated from their content assets.

Not every media company that desires to distribute content to multiple platforms is able to do so. To become a multi-platform media enterprise and stay competitive in a media marketplace where audiences have demand for cross-media content, some media companies choose to form strategic alliances to help with distribution. A strategic alliance is "a business relationship in which two or more companies, working to achieve a collective advantage, attempt to integrate operational functions, share risks, and align corporate cultures" (Chan-Olmsted, 1998, p. 34).

Strategic Alliances for Distribution Platforms

Allying with Internet ventures including web portals, niche websites, and Internet service providers is a widely adopted strategy among traditional media companies. For example, Hulu.com began as a joint venture between NBC Universal and News Corporation to launch the service, which became one of the most popular online TV websites in the U.S. Media companies use their alliances with Internet partners to increase their reach, acquire niche and new audiences, construct web properties, build cross-platform structures, and expand their brands (Liu & Chan-Olmsted, 2003).

A number of media companies have formed alliances with YouTube, the primary video-sharing website, with billions of subscribers worldwide, to distribute content over the Internet. These media companies offer "official" branded YouTube channels featuring full episodes of programs as well as video clips from their original programming on YouTube.

Media companies also engage in strategic alliances with companies that specialize in delivering digital content to different platforms. Technology companies provide the distribution channel, servers, and software that enable media companies to distribute content across different platforms. For example, thePlatform.com offers content providers services in broadband video management and publishing. On2 Technologies, a leading technology firm in digital video compression, has On2 Video compression and streaming technologies widely used in content delivery via the Internet, video on demand and mobile devices. Akamai Technologies, Inc., a leading service provider with comprehensive online media delivery and syndication technologies, has a global network optimized for delivery, streaming, and storage of digital media content.

These are examples of companies desired by multi-platform media enterprises because they are able to help distribute content across different platforms, enhance user experience, and thus increase the value of a media company's assets. A number of the leading U.S. cable operators including Comcast and Time Warner have formed strategic alliances with on-demand technology companies such as SeaChange International, Concurrent Computer Corporation, and iN DEMAND in order to develop VOD services. Viacom and Warner Music hold partnerships with Akamai Technologies to deliver online content to audiences via Akamai Technologies' delivery network. The official website for the U.S. White House utilizes Akamai Technologies for hosting video clips of the President's speeches and remarks.

Business Models

Media enterprises usually establish a revenue-sharing model in their alliances with Internet partners. The content providers take the majority of the revenues generated from online distribution, and their online partners receive a small percentage of the revenues, approximately 10%, depending on traffic that they can bring to the sites (Mahmud, 2007). Content providers can also sell advertising and embed messages in their

Table 5.2 Examples of New Business Models for Media Platforms

BUSINESS MODEL	EXAMPLES
Advertiser-supported	Embedded commercials, banner ads, click-through advertising.
Subscriptions	Annual, monthly, or weekly payments to receive premium content.
Pay-per-use	User pays only for content obtained. Can be used for music and videos (iTunes) or for archival content from newspapers, magazines, or broadcast sites.

Source: Author's compilation.

programs. Programs available through Hulu.com contain advertising, which allows the providers a means to capture some revenues from online viewing. For 2009, one analyst projects Hulu.com to generate about $120 million in advertising sales (Frommer, 2009).

Multi-platform media enterprises have been experimenting with different business models. The business models commonly adopted by multi-platform media enterprises include the advertising-based model, the subscription-based model, and in some cases a pay-per-use model (see Table 5.2).

In the advertising-based model, content is usually available free in exchange for advertisements placed within the content. Most media enterprises utilize the advertising-based business model on the Internet. According to the Interactive Advertising Bureau (IAB), Internet advertising revenue has increased from $4.6 billion in 1999 to $23.4 billion in 2008 (IAB, 2009b). However, this includes all forms of Internet advertising. Media companies have a considerable share of Internet advertising revenue. For example, the Newspaper Association of America (NAA) reported that the Internet advertising revenue of the newspaper industry was $3.1 billion in 2008 (NAA, 2009b).

In regard to other models, the *Wall Street Journal Online* (www. WSJ.com) is the best example of a successful subscription-based model. Readers pay an annual fee in order to gain full access to the list of headlines and articles featured on WSJ.com. The website does offer some free content on a trial basis, but in order to get the full content the user must have a subscription.

Subscription models can also be found in the mobile phone market space. Verizon Wireless provides V CAST Mobile TV, a subscription-based VOD service available on enabled phones. V CAST Mobile TV comprises short clips and promotional content as well as full-length commercial-free TV programs. V CAST Mobile TV subscribers can access programs from a number of networks and providers on their mobile phones, with revenue shared between Verizon and its partners.

Another emerging business model is known as simply "pay-per-use." In this model the consumer pays for a particular type of content rather than engaging in a regular subscription. One example is Apple's iTunes service, which allows users to purchase individual sound recordings, TV programs, and movies. As with other services, the content provider shares the revenues with the platform. In the case of iTunes, Apple takes a percentage of each recording sold, and the remainder goes to the holder of the original content, typically a record label in the case of music or a studio distributor for TV and movie content.

In addition, Anderson (2009) describes 50 business models based on some aspect of offering items (e.g., media content) for free. Not all of the models discussed in the author's book have relevance to the media industries, but several do. A few examples of these business models are detailed in Table 5.3.

Multi-platform media enterprises must balance their goal of making content available to consumers through different platforms with the goal of maximizing their assets. Channel conflict can be a potential problem for multi-platform media enterprises, especially those that use an advertising-based model. When a multi-platform media enterprise makes its content available on different platforms, these platforms in a sense compete against one another for audience time—which means these platforms compete against each other for advertising dollars.

Despite the business model employed, multi-platform content distribution requires media companies to coordinate their distribution

Table 5.3 Examples of Free Business Models

CATEGORY OF MODEL	EXAMPLES
Direct cross-subsidies	Free mobile phones, sell talk time.
	Free trial magazine/newspaper subscriptions, used to sell new subscriptions.
Three-party/two-sided markets (one class subsidizes another)	Free content in exchange for free advertising.
	Product placement in TV/movies (paid by advertisers).
Freemium (some customers subsidize others)	Give away web content, sell magazines/books.
	Give away music, sell music (iTunes).
	Give away book samples, sell books.

Source: Adapted from Anderson (2009).

efforts. Companies must integrate content distribution across different platforms in order to maximize efficiency. Some media enterprises have established a content distribution division especially to manage distribution. For example, Viacom's MTV Networks and BET Networks unit features a Content Distribution and Marketing Division that manages distribution of MTV Networks and BET Networks content to its partners including cable and satellite distributors, Internet ventures, mobile carriers, and other providers (Viacom's MTV Networks, 2007).

CASE STUDIES OF MULTI-PLATFORM MEDIA ENTERPRISES

In this section, four media enterprises, including the NBC network television hit program *Heroes*, the *Wall Street Journal*, BBC Radio, and a Dallas/Fort Worth, Texas television station, WFAA-TV, are used as representative case studies to illustrate how companies distribute content across multiple platforms. As these cases are presented, take note of the strategic elements involved as well as the potential business models the different platforms offer.

Case Study: NBC Universal's *Heroes*

On Monday, September 25, 2006, the program *Heroes* debuted and quickly became an audience favorite and one of NBC's highest-rated primetime programs. *Heroes* has won several awards and been nominated for both the Emmy and the Golden Globes.

As a breakout hit for the network, NBC has distributed *Heroes* and additional content across several platforms, expanding the program's presence, its audience reach, and the NBC Universal brand (see Figure 5.1). NBC offers full-length programs through the Internet (via nbc.com and hulu.com) and makes the entire series available for purchase on DVD. In addition, there is a large social media presence for *Heroes* via Twitter, Facebook, Digg, and even a *Heroes* Wiki (http://heroeswiki. com/Main_Page), where audience members can contribute to the discussion. *Heroes* can be found on other platforms, ranging from online and mobile games to music soundtracks, books and graphic novels, and merchandise to buy.

Making *Heroes* available across different platforms has several benefits for NBC and its viewers. For the network, the primary benefit is attracting and retaining viewers by providing multiple ways to stay connected with *Heroes* via various platforms. Just as importantly for the network, multi-platform distribution of *Heroes* increases the number of potential revenue sources, helping NBC monetize its digital content. And viewers and fans of the series can access *Heroes* from whichever

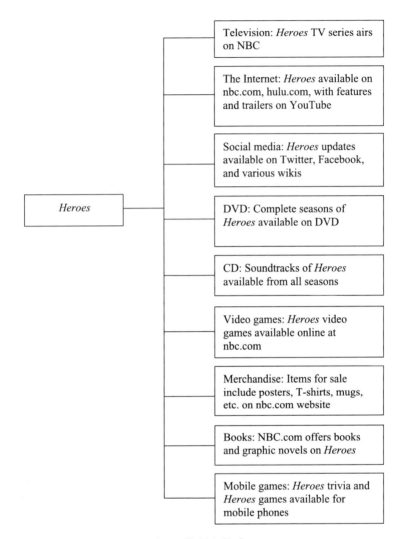

Figure 5.1   NBC Universal's *Heroes* Across Multiple Platforms

Source: Compiled by the author from numerous sources.

platform they would like and have access to, and consume the content whenever and wherever they want.

Case Study: The *Wall Street Journal*

The *Wall Street Journal* is the most recognized business publication in the world, and also distributes content to multiple platforms. In 2007, the assets of the *Wall Street Journal* and parent company Dow Jones

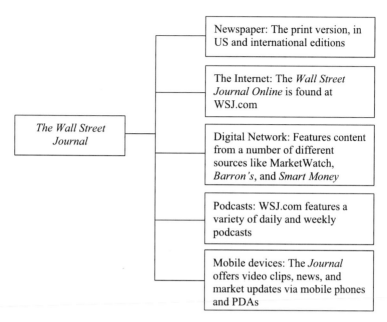

Figure 5.2 The *Wall Street Journal*'s Distribution Platforms

Source: Author's compilation.

were acquired by News Corporation in a $5 billion acquisition. The *Wall Street Journal*'s website (www.WSJ.com) features full text of the print journal's various editions along with many premium features on a subscription basis. The Wall Street Journal Digital Network enhanced features include video, interactive features, blogs, forums, archived articles from daily editions of the *Wall Street Journal* for the previous 90 days, and other content. Advanced searching of the archives is available for an additional fee. In addition to the Internet, the *Wall Street Journal* distributes content via mobile phones, podcasts, and RSS feeds.

The Wall Street Journal Digital Network is found on the website, and offers additional content from MarketWatch, *Barron's* (also owned by News Corporation), All Things Digital, and *Smart Money* (a magazine owned by News Corporation). There is a variety of blogs available through the website, as well as a section called Journal Community, which is an open forum for discussion on a number of topics. Podcasts can be accessed via WSJ.com and other websites including iTunes, my.Yahoo, and my.Google. The *Wall Street Journal* casts its videos, podcasts, and the latest news specifically formatted for mobile users and updated throughout the day to mobile devices, but is scheduled to begin charging for its mobile applications in 2010. A look at the *Wall Street Journal*'s use of multiple platforms is found in Figure 5.2.

Case Study: BBC Radio

The British Broadcasting Corporation (BBC) is one of the world's oldest and most admired media enterprises. The BBC uses a variety of platforms to distribute its content to audiences around the world. Here we will examine one division of the company, BBC Radio (http://www.bbc.co.uk/radio/), to understand how this segment uses multiple distribution platforms. In addition to its terrestrial broadcasts, BBC Radio also delivers its content through the Internet, mobile devices (phones and PDAs), an iPlayer, and a wide variety of podcasts.

The numerous BBC Radio channels are available online, including all of its national radio stations, the BBC World Service, and specific-

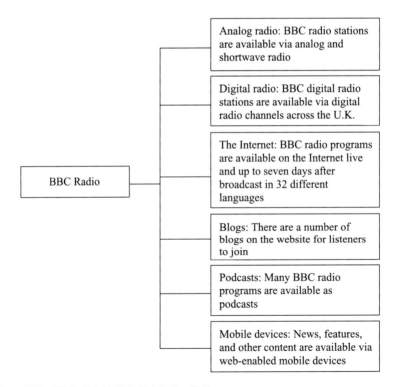

Figure 5.3   BBC Radio's Multiple Distribution Platforms

Source: Author's compilation.

country radio services (Scotland, Ulster, Wales, etc.). All of the division's national, local, and regional stations are available live on the Internet, and most of its radio programs are available on the Internet for up to seven days after their original broadcast. Further, the information is available in up to 32 different languages.

BBC Radio hosts a number of blogs on a variety of topics of interest to listeners. A look at the various distribution platforms for BBC is found in Figure 5.3.

Case Study: WFAA-TV

WFAA-TV is the flagship television station owned by the Belo Corp. WFAA is an ABC network affiliate serving the Dallas/Fort Worth, Texas market, ranked as the fifth-largest media market in the U.S. WFAA distributes local information and entertainment content through its website (www.wfaa.com). At the website, users can sign up for a number of platforms on which they can receive content and other information (see Figure 5.4). Among the options are a number of RSS news feeds including Latest News, From News 8, News 8 Investigates, and Local News. The station also offers information for access on mobile phones and PDAs. The station has a large presence with social

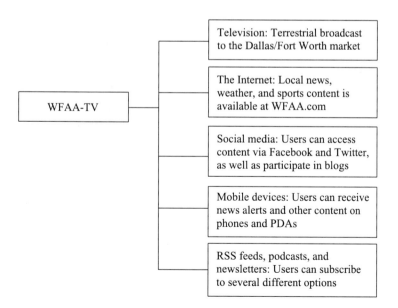

Figure 5.4 WFAA-TV's Multiple Platforms

Source: Compiled by the author from wfaa.com.

media, with accounts on both Facebook and Twitter. The station also has a number of blogs for users to participate in and comment on. The station provides several email updates for users to access via their computer or mobile device.

These four case studies illustrate how media enterprises use a number of different distribution platforms to deliver content to audiences. The size and type of the media company and the nature of the content to be delivered to some extent decide what platforms or devices are used by a media company for content distribution. Large media conglomerates such as NBC Universal (part of General Electric) and the *Wall Street Journal* (owned by News Corporation) utilize the most platforms in very sophisticated ways, no doubt because they have considerable resources to develop a multi-platform content distribution strategy and can cross-promote these platforms via their other holdings and media brands.

In the case of BBC Radio, the division draws on the larger resources of the parent British Broadcasting Corporation to provide a truly global radio experience. While the content is entirely audio-based, the wide number of available platforms and the number of languages in which content is offered add to the utility for the consumer. In contrast, WFAA-TV uses fewer content distribution platforms but in a more targeted way, geared toward an emphasis on local news and weather information important to its market. WFAA-TV is not concerned about a national or international reach; instead the television station is offering content primarily designed for the local audience around the station's geographical market.

Regardless of the size and scope of the media enterprise, in order to have a multi-platform strategy there must be: a strong Internet presence to attract users connecting via a computer; a mobile strategy to attract users with phones and PDAs; podcasts and videocasts to share content in smaller forms and formats; a social media strategy to create interaction and build "community" among audience members; and some sort of blogging strategy to promote online discussion and feedback. Ultimately, all media enterprises hope to monetize their various platforms, whether through advertising, subscriptions, or some sort of pay-per-use model. Getting consumers to recognize the value in these platforms and their willingness to pay will be an ongoing challenge for media enterprises.

SUMMARY

In the 21st century, media companies are best understood as enterprises distributing content (information and entertainment) to multiple platforms and devices. The transition to multi-platform media enterprises has been driven by technology, audiences' changing behaviors and adoption of new technology, and demand for cross-platform content. The chapter introduced 21 different platforms in use by media companies as of late 2009. No doubt, more platforms are in development as technology constantly upgrades and evolves. In addition to looking at the various platforms, the chapter also examined consumers as multi-platform users.

The chapter reviewed strategies and business models of media enterprises. In terms of strategy, many media companies have formed strategic alliances with other technology partners to develop new distribution platforms. As for business models, most media enterprises are using advertising, subscriptions, or pay-per-use. Free business models were also reviewed in terms of their application to the media industries. Regardless which business model is used, multi-platform media enterprises need to coordinate content distribution across different platforms to avoid channel conflict.

The chapter concluded by looking at four different case studies to illustrate how media enterprises use multiple platforms to distribute content. These examples indicate that media companies' choices of content distribution platforms differ owing to the size and type of media companies and the nature of the content to be delivered.

Multi-platform content distribution will continue to expand and evolve in the 21st century. Likewise, we will continue to see the evolution of business models employed in multi-platform content distribution that will likely take on more scope and complexity. Multi-platform media enterprises represent an important developing aspect of the media economy. With more innovations in content distribution platforms and consumer technology, a multi-platform distribution strategy used in conjunction with a variety of business models has become a required way of doing business in the media economy.

DISCUSSION QUESTIONS

1. Why is it necessary to think of media firms as multi-platform enterprises in the 21st century?
2. Which of the many platforms available to reach consumers have the most promise? Which platforms do you think have the least promise?

3. How do you use different platforms available for information and entertainment content? Which platforms do you like? Are there any that you dislike? Why?

4. The chapter discusses strategies and business models associated with multiple distribution platforms. Pick a local media company in the area where you live and analyze how it is using various platforms from both a strategy and a business model perspective.

5. In reviewing the case studies involving *Heroes*, the *Wall Street Journal*, BBC Radio, and WFAA-TV, what do you find as similarities among these companies and their strategies? What do you identify as the differences among these companies and their strategies?

CHAPTER 6

Technology and the Media Economy

In this chapter you will learn:

- why technology is a force impacting the media economy;
- how the transition from analog to digital technology impacted the media industries;
- how broadband development not only offers high-speed access to the Internet but also plays a role in GDP;
- how satellites changed the media industries and the ability to deliver content;
- pitfalls associated with technological development from the perspective of society, business, and consumers.

Technology is one of the main drivers of the media economy. In the history of the media industries, a number of distribution and reception technologies have enhanced as well as disrupted the media economy. As seen in Chapter 5, technology impacts the processes involved in production, distribution, and exhibition of media products as well as how audiences receive and use media products. The introduction of transistors and the introduction of integrated circuits were major milestones in developing new technology across many types of business and industry, along with the ability to create faster and faster processors used in computers and computing technology.

Technology impacts how media firms and industries function across different levels of activity of the media economy, ranging from the individual through the household, national, and global levels. In the 21st century, numerous innovations in content distribution and reception technology have emerged. Perhaps the key catalyst was the transition from analog-based systems to digital technology, built on binary code, which was created in the 17th century. Digital technology became widespread in the 1980s, and has been applied to production, distribution, and exhibition of media products since that time.

This chapter analyzes technology and its impact on the media economy. In the following sections, analyses are provided of: 1) the transition from analog to digital; 2) the development of broadband; 3) satellite technology; and 4) pitfalls of digital technology. Individual case studies will be presented within these sections to illustrate trends and patterns.

THE TRANSITION FROM ANALOG TO DIGITAL

Digital technology is revolutionary to media firms and industries because of the way it transforms production, distribution, and exhibition of media products. With analog technology, an audio or video signal is processed into electronic pulses; with digital technology, audio or video signal is translated into patterns of numbers where the audio or video data is represented by a series of "digits" made up of binary code—referring to combinations of the numbers "0" and "1" (Negroponte, 1996). Digital content has a number of advantages over analog content, including enhanced sound and picture quality, improved reception, and the ability to be repurposed and repackaged across a number of different platforms.

In addition to quality issues, digital technology provides other benefits. Equipment is smaller owing to digital technology, can be produced more cheaply, and has greater capacity. Analog material can be preserved better in a digital format, although the conversion from analog to digital becomes more complex and requires more capacity when moving from a simple item like text and still photographs to audio, video, and motion picture files.

Media firms and industries in most parts of the globe are nearly complete in the process of transitioning from analog to digital so that they can deliver content with better audio and video quality to audiences. Some media industries have already adopted digital technology for content creation, production, distribution, and exhibition. For example, in the United States the radio industry introduced HD radio technology in 2005, the broadcast television industry converted to digital television in June 2009, the cable television industry began upgrading cable systems to digital in the 1990s, and the motion picture industry has embraced digital distribution and exhibition of television programs and movies. Let's examine in more detail one example of a transition from analog to digital, using the development and introduction of HD (high density) radio in the United States.

Case Study: The Introduction of HD Radio in the United States

The creation of HD radio in the United States is used as an example to illustrate the transition to digital technology. HD radio technology was originally developed by iBiquity Digital Corporation, and was approved by the Federal Communications Commission (FCC) as the only digital audio broadcasting standard in the United States in October 2002. HD radio allows radio stations to offer digital audio sub-channels along with their traditional analog channels on AM/FM, thereby providing outlets to reach new audiences and grow new revenue streams. For consumers, a new receiver is required to receive HD radio signals, as the signals are not currently compatible with existing AM/FM receivers. However, one application has been introduced for the Apple iPhone that allows reception of HD radio signals (*HD radio on your iPhone?*, 2009).

HD radio is considered the most revolutionary technology in radio broadcasting since the introduction of FM stereo in the 1960s (*HD radio broadcasting fact sheet*, 2009). With HD radio, AM and FM radio stations can extend their markets and reach. In addition, stations can offer text information such as real-time title and artist identification, and traffic, weather, and stock information directly to HD receivers.

iBiquity Digital Corporation formed a partnership with the major broadcast equipment manufacturers in order to accelerate the commercial development of products based on HD radio technology. The advances in HD technology have greatly reduced the size and costs of transmission equipment, and thus facilitated the transition to broadcasting in HD. Many radio stations have upgraded their facilities to broadcast with the HD radio technology. As of the end of 2009, HD radio was available to over 85% of the U.S. population, with 1,950 HD radio stations broadcasting in the United States (*Find HD radio stations*, 2009). As would be expected, the largest U.S. commercial radio groups (e.g., Clear Channel, CBS, Cumulus, Citadel, etc.) are among the biggest groups offering HD channels with their existing stations.

In addition to the United States, other countries that have adopted HD radio as of 2009 include Brazil, Mexico, and the Philippines. Countries involved in testing and demonstrations of HD radio include Canada, China, Colombia, Germany, Indonesia, Jamaica, New Zealand, Poland, Switzerland, Thailand, and Ukraine, with other countries in development (*HD radio broadcasting fact sheet*, 2009). We can expect greater development and diffusion of HD radio over the next decade, as the availability of HD radio stations grows, the cost of HD receivers declines, and HD becomes a standard in many new automobiles.

BROADBAND DEVELOPMENT

Broadband refers to connections that enable users to access the Internet at speeds of at least 256 kilobytes per second or higher. Broadband Internet services have become more accessible and affordable since the late 1990s, first via digital subscriber lines (DSL), followed by higher-speed cable modems and later by fiber/local area networks (e.g., IPTV) delivered by telecommunication companies like Verizon and AT&T, and some cable operators like Comcast and Time Warner. A growing market in the 21st century will be wireless broadband, primarily received via smart phones and netbook computers. Increasing competition in the home broadband Internet access service market has lowered the price of broadband services worldwide.

Broadband penetration rates continue to increase on a global basis. Table 6.1 illustrates how a sample of the G-20 nations (identified in Chapter 1) compare in terms of broadband penetration, the total number of broadband subscribers, and GDP per capita at purchasing power parity (PPP). The information on broadband penetration rates and the total number of broadband subscribers of the 11 nations was obtained from the Organisation for Economic Co-operation and Development (OECD) and the CIA *World Factbook* (2009b). It should be noted that data was not available on all of the G-20 nations, so only those countries

Table 6.1 A Look at Global Broadband Penetration (2008)

COUNTRY	BROADBAND PENETRATION (%)	BROADBAND SUBSCRIBERS	GDP PER CAP (IN USD)
Canada	28.6	9,577,648	$39,100
France	27.6	17,725,000	$33,200
Germany	27.3	22,532,000	$35,400
Italy	19.4	11,283,000	$31,300
Japan	23.6	30,107,327	$34,000
UK	28.2	17,275,660	$36,500
USA	25.2	77,437,868	$46,900
China	6.2	83,400,000	$6,000
Brazil	5.0	10,000,000	$10,200
Mexico	6.8	7,604,629	$14,200
Australia	25.2	5,368,000	$38,100
South Korea	31.9	15,474,931	$27,600
Turkey	7.4	5,736,619	$11,900

Sources: Compiled from CIA (2009b); International Telecommunications Union (2009); Market Research (2009); OECD (2008).

in which comparative data could be obtained are listed in Table 6.1. All data in Table 6.1 is based on the year 2008.

Among the nations listed in Table 6.1, South Korea leads with a broadband penetration rate of 31.9%, followed by Canada, the United Kingdom, France, and Germany. Brazil, China, Mexico, and Turkey all have broadband penetration rates of less than 10%. In terms of the total number of broadband subscribers, China ranks first with 83.4 million broadband subscribers, followed by the United States, Japan, Germany, and France.

PPP GDP per capita is used in the table as it takes into account differences in the relative prices of goods and services and is a better measure for comparing global economies. A simple Pearson correlation was run by the author using broadband penetration rate (expressed as a percentage) and GDP per capita, resulting in a highly positive correlation of +.879. This shows that broadband penetration and GDP per capita are highly correlated, indicating that higher levels of broadband penetration contribute positively to a nation's GDP. This analysis suggests that large emerging economies such as Brazil, China, and Mexico will continue to see accelerated growth in GDP as a result of greater investment in broadband.

SATELLITE TECHNOLOGY

Satellite communication technology began in the 1950s when both the former Soviet Union and the United States launched their first satellites. The satellite became one of the most important technologies in media history and today allows us to be transported around the world at a moment's notice. Satellite technology positively impacted the development of many media industries such as cable television, telecommunications, satellite radio, and direct broadcast satellites (DBS). In the 1970s, pay-cable networks (e.g., Home Box Office, Showtime) and superstations (e.g., WTBS, Atlanta; WGN, Chicago; WOR, New York) embraced domestic satellite transmission to relay television programming to cable systems, giving households more reasons to subscribe to the nascent cable TV services. With satellite communication technology, the cable industry acquired a substantial number of subscribers and established itself as a competitive force in the video programming market. In the 21st century, total viewing of satellite-delivered channels routinely outperforms that of programming originating on the four major broadcast networks.

Satellite technology introduced a new means to distribute content directly to consumers, leading to DBS services like DirecTV and Dish, enabling these start-ups to compete in the multichannel video programming market with cable and telecommunications companies. In the radio industry, the development of satellite radio introduced a powerful new competitor to the terrestrial radio industry. In both cases, DBS and satellite radio provided audiences with more programming and platform choices. A case study on satellite radio provides additional details.

Case Study: Satellite Radio
In 1997, the FCC finally granted licenses to XM Satellite Radio and Sirius Satellite Radio to offer the first digital audio radio services (DARS) to subscribers. For many years, radio companies had successfully lobbied against satellite radio, delaying the technology's entry into the market. XM debuted on September 25, 2001; Sirius debuted on July 1, 2002. Both services were subscription-based services, and also offered some premium content in addition to regular packages. XM and Sirius were allowed to combine in a controversial merger in 2008 to save costs, with the new entity known as Sirius XM Radio. The entities were able to convince regulators that if they were not allowed to merge it was likely both services could go out of business.

Sirius XM offers advantages over terrestrial radio, including digital sound quality, national coverage, and enhanced programming choices. The service offers over 100 channels of commercial-free music, news, talk, and sports programming in packages to subscribers for a monthly fee. Sirius XM is also available for subscription through the Internet, and via an iPhone application.

Sirius XM competes with traditional radio for listeners, as well as Internet radio, and users who listen to music on their iPod/Mp3 players or their mobile phones. The recession of 2008–2009 hurt Sirius XM in that fewer automobiles were sold, a major source of new subscriptions. In addition, as consumers began to lose jobs and homes, discretionary spending tightened considerably. Despite the high quality and variety of programming options, there are questions as to the long-term economic viability of Sirius XM. International expansion is one option, as the company hopes to expand beyond its present footprint, which covers the United States, Canada, and Puerto Rico. Internet and smart phone subscriptions are also seen as important areas to grow revenue streams.

PITFALLS OF TECHNOLOGY
Technology offers many conveniences and enhancements for media firms and consumers, but not all of the impact is positive. This section

of the chapter details three areas where technology has created challenges for business and industry as well as society. These include the costs of upgrading technology, the impact on piracy on intellectual property, and social concerns caused by technology.

Upgrading Technology

Technology enables media firms to distribute content to various platforms with improved sound and picture quality in a high-speed broadband environment. At the same time, technology requires firms operating in the media economy to make constant investments to keep up with changing technology. For example, since the passage of the Telecommunications Act of 1996, the U.S. cable industry has invested well over $150 billion in upgrading its facilities to meet the rising demand for broadband applications such as digital television, video on demand, and interactive program guides (IPGs).

For "suppliers" of media content, technology expenses can be categorized in three main areas:

- *Infrastructure and networking expenses*. These are expenses related to the actual physical plant of distributing content, either by terrestrial, broadband, satellite, or other means.
- *Hardware and software*. These are the expenses assigned to the actual production of the content, which must be recaptured in the marketplace. Hardware refers to equipment such as cameras, lighting, and studios, and software refers to editing and post-production tools needed to finish rough cuts and works in progress.
- *License, talent, and other fees*. These fees range from fees for the use of copyrighted materials such as music to the cost of hiring production personnel and talent to other fees not covered in the other categories.

The upgrading of technology is also felt by audiences and individual consumers. In this respect there are two main categories of consumer expenses:

- *Costs to adopt new technology*. The cost for new technology is usually high during its first few months of entry into the market, but often drops as more and more consumers adopt. In the 1980s when personal computers were introduced, costs for a desktop system could easily exceed $2,000 depending on the

brand. In the 21st century, you can buy a complete desktop
system for under $500.

- *Cost to upgrade software and hardware.* Technology has to be
upgraded in order to maintain its functionality, whether in
regard to the physical hardware (e.g., PCs, laptops, video game
consoles, DVRs, etc.) or the software that runs the various
applications. While some initial upgrades may be offered for free
by the vendor, most upgrading involves replacing hardware every
two to three years and software whenever new versions make old
versions obsolete.

For example, the video cassette dominated the home video market
until the 1990s when DVD technology was introduced. Consumers
purchased new hardware (DVD players) and new software (the DVDs
themselves) as movie studios gradually stopped releasing new titles to
video cassettes. The audience experience was enhanced with the DVD
because of better sound and video quality, additional features, and
expanded content. Blu-ray represents the latest innovation in the DVD
market. The Sony product provides enhanced audio and high-definition
video over standard DVD, and other features not available on standard
DVD technology.

One of the best examples of upgrading technology in contemporary
times involves the transition to digital television (DTV), which involves
costs for both the media industries and individuals. Let's examine the
DTV transition in the U.S. in the following case study.

Case Study: The Digital Television Transition in the United States
Mandated by Congress during the 1990s, the switch to DTV was finally
realized in June 2009 following several years of delays and
postponements. In the U.S. there are two DTV formats: standard-
definition TV (SDTV) and high-definition TV (HDTV). HDTV has the
highest resolution and picture quality among DTV formats.

In terms of costs, the broadcast television industry spent billions of
dollars to upgrade its technology for the transition to digital and the
capability to offer HDTV. There were costs for new transmitters,
cameras, switchers, field equipment, and editing facilities to handle the
new digital standard.

The federal government also spent millions of dollars on the
transition in two distinct ways. First, a DTV awareness campaign was
conducted across the entire country to inform consumers about the
DTV transition; the campaign involved multimedia approaches using

the Internet, printed materials, public service announcements, and even paid advertising. Second, the National Telecommunications and Information Administration (NTIA) distributed tens of thousands of discounted coupons to purchase a converter set top box for consumers with old analog receivers. The program actually ran out of coupons at one point in the spring of 2009, only to issue thousands more in a second wave prior to the DTV transition in June of that year.

Consumers had three options to prepare for the DTV transition, but all involved some form of expense. First, if the consumer already subscribed to a cable, satellite, or IPTV service, their existing converter box would handle the digital transition through their monthly subscription. While these consumers had to do nothing, they were still paying a monthly fee for television content. Second, consumers with an analog TV set who were not subscribers either had to replace their old set with a digital tuner or had to acquire a set top converter box. Millions of consumers chose to replace their old analog sets with new receivers that were also capable of receiving HDTV signals. Third, thousands more consumers opted to obtain a converter box (ideally with an NTIA coupon) for their old analog sets, which provided the cheapest way to receive digital television without purchasing a new digital tuner.

Countries around the globe are in different phases of DTV transition. A few countries, such as Finland, Austria, and Switzerland, have already completed the process. Canada is on track to convert in 2011, while the United Kingdom plans to complete the switchover by 2012.

Intellectual Property Issues

Innovations in media technology present a plethora of intellectual property issues. The World Intellectual Property Organization (WIPO) defines intellectual property as "creations of the mind: inventions, literary and artistic works, and symbols, names, images, and designs used in commerce" (WIPO, 2009). Intellectual property can be classified into two categories: industrial property, which includes patents, trademarks, industrial designs, and geographic indications of source; and copyright, which includes literary and artistic works (WIPO, 2009). Copyright is therefore dominant in the media industries, since firms produce information and entertainment products.

Virtually all media content involves copyrights, ranging across film and television content, sound recordings, books and other forms of print, software and operating systems for computers, and video games.

Global piracy poses a serious economic threat to U.S. media industries because they produce most of the information and entertainment products in the world. The United States is the world's largest exporter of copyright-based products, and thus is the most directly affected by increasing global copyright piracy. According to an analysis by the Institute for Policy Innovation (Siwek, 2007), global copyright piracy costs the U.S. economy an estimated $58.0 billion in total output a year, along with an estimated loss of 373,375 jobs, $16.3 billion loss in workers' earnings, and $2.58 billion loss in tax revenues (see Table 6.2).

Trade-Related Aspects of Intellectual Property Rights (TRIPS) is an international agreement administered by the World Trade Organization (WTO). In TRIPS, minimum standards for intellectual property regulation are specified. The TRIPS agreement is used by many countries as a basic legal framework for intellectual property regulation. However, enforcing intellectual property regulation globally is extremely challenging because some countries are not willing either to commit resources or to take action to protect intellectual property rights (U.S. Copyright Office, 2005). Copyright piracy rates are extremely high in some European and Asian countries, especially in Russia, China, and Thailand, to name just a few.

The availability of broadband technology naturally leads to higher Internet piracy rates, especially in countries with high piracy rates. Internet piracy, according to the Motion Picture Association of America, involves the downloading or distribution of unauthorized copies of intellectual property via the Internet, including all types of content (e. g., movies, sound recordings, video games, etc.). Internet piracy can take various forms, including peer-to-peer (P2P) file-sharing networks, pirate servers, and illegal websites. These forms of Internet piracy have

Table 6.2   The Cost of Global Piracy to the U.S. Economy (2005)

	ECONOMIC LOSSES (BILLIONS/USD)	JOBS LOST	LOSS IN WORKERS' EARNINGS (BILLIONS/USD)		LOSS IN TAX REVENUES (BILLIONS/USD)
Production level	52.4	312,052	14.6	Personal income	1.76
Retail level	5.6	61,323	1.7	Corporate income	0.56
				Production and other taxes	0.26
Total	58.0	373,375	16.3	Total	2.58

Source: Siwek (2007).

greatly accelerated global copyright piracy. P2P services have made the enforcement of intellectual property regulation more complicated and difficult than at any time in history.

As seen in Table 6.2, technology clearly harms the potential revenue streams of media firms and industries, which in turn impacts a nation's economy. The recording industry has been the most impacted by piracy. With the Internet, illegal distributing and sharing of music are easy. Downloading pirated music from the Internet has become rampant, enabled by technology.

In order to protect intellectual property rights, media industries have pursued numerous lawsuits against individuals for copyright violations, as well as large-scale anti-piracy campaigns. Some media firms try to thwart digital copyright piracy by offering affordable, easy-to-use legal download services. To discourage people from consuming pirated music, record companies have licensed a number of partners offering download services including Internet streaming, legitimate P2P services, and audio and video downloads.

Social Concerns

Technology has generated some social concerns, such as the problems associated with the digital divide and social isolation caused by excessive use of computers and other forms of technology. The digital divide refers to the gap between those who have access to digital technology and those who do not. The digital divide can be analyzed along two dimensions: the gap in physical access to digital technology and the gap in resources and skills required to effectively use digital technology. Many factors contribute to the inequality in access to digital technology, including socioeconomic status, race, education, gender, age, income, and others. People who do not have access to digital technology cannot benefit from information technology, which has become a key component of the educational, economic, and social sectors of some economies.

The global digital divide refers to differences in access to digital technology among countries. The global digital divide poses many challenges for countries with slower development and emerging economies. Despite an increase in broadband Internet penetration rate worldwide, the digital divide between developed countries and emerging markets continues to grow. Billions of people in emerging markets realize no benefit from the promises of technology owing to the lack of access to digital technology. Various factors may have contributed to the gap in consumer Internet adoption among countries. Regulatory institutions, educational systems, industrialization, economic institutions, and national culture all influence consumer Internet adoption (Zhao, Kim, Suh, & Du, 2007). Owing to the importance of digital technology in economic development, governments, the private sector, non-profit organizations, and financial institutions around the world are working to bridge the global digital divide. Some smaller nations, such as Uruguay and Bolivia, are providing laptops with Internet access to elementary school children in order to get them acclimated to using technology.

Another social concern regarding technology is that involving excessive usage of computers, games, Internet surfing, and social networks, which can lead to social isolation, not to mention health concerns. With more programming choices, platform choices, and features available, audiences are spending more time with media than ever before, and data in Chapter 9 details how consumers are spending time with various forms of media and technology. Increases in media and technology usage reduce people's involvement in social life, including informal social interaction, attending public events, participating in civic activities, attending church and other institutions, and perhaps most importantly exercising.

Some social critics posit that excessive usage of technology leads to people's disengagement in their social life, based on the assumption that time spent with digital technology displaces social activities and creates a psychological barrier to people participating in social activities (Shah, Schmierbach, Hawkins, Espino, & Donavan, 2002). Excessive Internet usage has especially concerned social critics. A number of studies were conducted to investigate the impact of Internet usage on people's engagement in social life. Some of these studies indicate that excessive Internet usage disengages people from meaningful social relationships and community activities (Patterson & Kraut, 1998).

SUMMARY

This chapter has looked broadly at the role of technology as one of the primary forces impacting all levels of the media economy. Technology has had a profound impact on the processes involved in the creation, production, distribution, and exhibition of media products, and on consumers through reception technologies.

The transition from analog to digital technology revolutionized how media firms and industries provide entertainment and information to the individual, household, national, and global levels of the media economy. Digital technology enables media firms and industries to provide content with better audio and video quality, distribute content across multiple platforms in a faster manner, and give audiences more choices and control over how content is received and consumed.

Broadband development was also reviewed in the chapter. Broadband refers to a network system offering speeds of at least 256 kilobytes per second, and is made available via digital subscriber lines, cable modems, fiber/LAN, and wireless. Broadband was examined from a global perspective, with data illustrating that broadband penetration is highly correlated with GDP per capita.

Satellite communications were reviewed to demonstrate how this technology has not only shrunk the globe but made numerous channels of television programming available via cable, satellite, and IPTV services. A case study on Sirius XM satellite radio was also presented in the chapter.

The chapter reviewed three concerns with technology. The cost to upgrade technology was reviewed from the perspective both of media firms and of consumers. Piracy and intellectual property issues were also examined, with data from one study illustrating how billions of dollars and thousands of jobs are harmed by piracy, which is enabled by technological advances. Finally, social concerns involving the digital divide among nations at the global level, as well as social isolation of people with excessive media and technology usage at the individual level, were examined.

As a main driver of the media economy, technology interacts with other forces including globalization, regulation, and social aspects of the media economy. Together these forces shape both the contemporary and the future media economies around the world. Technology will continue to impact and influence the media economy at all levels of operation, forcing both media industries and consumers constantly to adapt to change and evolution.

DISCUSSION QUESTIONS

1. What are some of the advantages digital technology offers over the old analog technology?
2. How do we define broadband? How does broadband correlate with a nation's GDP? If broadband spurs economic growth, why don't governments spend more money to invest in their broadband infrastructure?
3. How did the development of satellite technology aid the expansion of other media-related industries like cable television and telecommunications companies?

4. What is the digital divide? What do you see as possible solutions to this global problem?
5. Piracy is a huge issue impacting the media economy. How does piracy impact the economic viability of media firms and media employment? What steps do you think could be taken by governments, media industries, and individuals to curb piracy?

CHAPTER 7

Globalization and the Media Economy

In this chapter you will learn:

- how to define globalization;
- which trade blocs and agreements are used to enhance globalization;
- why the media industries seek to globalize, and the types of products that are distributed in the global economy;
- which global strategies are used by media companies desiring to enter the world marketplace;
- the role of transnational media conglomerates (TRMCs) in globalization.

Another driving force in the media economy is globalization. The word "globalization" is value-laden, as it carries with it many different meanings and possible interpretations. From an academic perspective, globalization differs depending on what discipline is analyzing the phenomenon. For example, a political scientist interested in governmental policies and strategies would look at globalization differently than would someone in the natural sciences studying global warming and climate change. A historian would have a different focus than a scholar in sociology or in anthropology.

WHAT IS GLOBALIZATION?

Regardless of the perspective used in examining globalization, some consensus exists on some of the things that globalization means. First, globalization is an extension of the nation-state system. That is to say, when a country or nation decides to "globalize," it is typically centered on trade and commerce with other countries, importing needed scarce resources and exporting abundant resources. Globalization is a key aspect of the world's aggregate gross domestic product, manifested by the formation of the World Trade Organization (WTO) in 1995. According to the website www.globalization101.org, foreign investment has increased by 20 times since 1950, and from 1997 to 1999 flows of foreign investment grew from $468 billion to $827 billion (*What is globalization?*, n.d.).

A second core meaning of globalization is usually associated with a global system of military alliances. For example, the formation of the North Atlantic Treaty Organization (NATO) was designed to promote peace among nations by creating a strong military defense system among member countries to protect them from outside aggression, and to be a deterrent to future wars. The United Nations is another entity that provides some military support—typically in peacekeeping efforts—as well as working to ensure rights to all citizens of the globe.

Globalization is a force that in reality has existed for centuries—driven primarily by trade and commerce across nations (Micklethwait & Woolridge, 2000). But globalization became a much stronger force, especially during the last 30 years of the 20th century from 1970 to 2000 (Friedman, 2005). It was during this time frame that several significant events contributed to globalization, with much greater awareness of how the world had changed. Here are just a few of the significant events that demonstrated how the world had transformed:

- A global oil crisis in 1974 illustrated the world's dependence on crude oil, and high prices resulted from the impact of limited supply and insatiable demand for gasoline.
- The globe suffered a series of financial crises during the 1980s, beginning with the failures of a number of Japanese banks, followed by the U.S. savings and loan crisis in the mid-1980s. In October 1987 the global economy was shaken by devastating losses across the globe's financial markets, indicating the interdependence of the global financial institutions. Another painful global recession would hit nearly 20 years later, beginning in December 2007.
- Communism collapsed in 1989 with the symbolic fall of the Berlin Wall, coupled with many former Eastern European nations abandoning the Communist system in favor of a mixed economy driven by capitalism ideals. The Soviet Union would eventually break up.
- As more nations adapted to capitalism, economic activity in

trade and commerce increased, leading to the development of trade blocs such as the European Union and the North American Free Trade Agreement (NAFTA), and the creation of the WTO.
- Information technology improved and expanded communication and media use among nations, fueled by innovations like the fax machine, electronic mail, the Internet, and mobile phones. These technologies not only changed how people share information, but fueled business and investment activities. Perhaps the major technological impact has been the increasing speed at which information moves.

Positive and Negative Aspects of Globalization

Globalization is interpreted as both a positive and a negative force. In terms of positive aspects, globalization encourages competition for goods and services, spurs productivity, and in theory helps to keep prices low for consumers and raises the standard of living, especially in smaller countries. Globalization also factors in developing fresh ideas and innovation in numerous areas, ranging from agriculture to information technology. Finally, globalization is considered a positive force in that it helps to promote awareness and appreciation of other cultures.

Globalization is likewise criticized as a negative force. While criticisms range across a full gamut of possibilities, most concern centers around the development of global political institutions (e.g., the European Union) and global economic institutions (e.g., WTO, the World Bank, the International Monetary Fund). Another criticism is that globalization has led to an international free market dominated by large multinational corporations at the expense of local, indigenous enterprises. But probably the main criticism of globalization is that it has created a homogeneous global culture strongly influenced originally by the West, overshadowing the local culture and its customs (e.g., Sparks, 2007). Most of this criticism is tied directly to media content products (e.g., movies, TV programs, sound recordings) and advertising, which of course are heavily influenced by U.S. brands and content.

TRADE BLOCS AND AGREEMENTS

Global commerce is one of the key components of globalization. Central to this is the formation of trade blocs and agreements among countries to facilitate trade and commerce. The World Trade Organization estimated there were over 120 different trade agreements in existence in 2009; many countries belong to multiple trade blocs. The WTO tracks data and other trends among its member countries and provides a wealth of information on its website (http://www.wto.org) to aid researchers in understanding globalization trends.

Among the most important trade blocs are the European Union, which as of 2009 consisted of 27 nations, the North American Free Trade Agreement (Canada, Mexico, and the United States), and Asia-Pacific Economic Cooperation (APEC), which has over 20 member nations. In fact, an estimated 80% of global GDP comes from these three regions of the world, known as the triad (Chan-Olmsted & Albarran, 1998). As of 2007, which has the most complete listing of available global data from the WTO, these three trade blocs represented over half of all global trade in 2007.

As seen in Figure 7.1, the European Union is the largest trade bloc in the world, with a combined $83 billion in imports and exports in 2007, followed by APEC with just over $50 billion, and finally NAFTA with approximately $30 billion. Notice also the discrepancy between imports and exports in the graph; we see the APEC group with a positive trade balance (greater exports than imports), while the EU and NAFTA have negative trade balances, although NAFTA's balance is larger than the EU's. APEC's positive trade balance is influenced by a number of factors, including the bloc's lower costs of production.

While these three trade blocs are the largest, there are other significant trade blocs that help facilitate global trade across the globe. Four other important blocs are the Association of Southeast Asian Nations (ASEAN), the Central European Free Trade Agreement (CEFTA), and two in Latin American, the Southern Common Market (in Spanish translated as MERCOSUR) and the Andean trade bloc.

In addition to trade blocs, other factors are also important in aiding

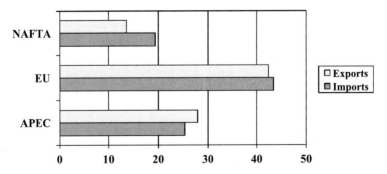

Figure 7.1 Imports and Exports Among the World's Largest Trade Blocs (Billions USD), 2007

Source: World Trade Organization.

globalization. Among these are the rise of global standards, privatization, disintegrating borders, competition, technology, demand for global products and customers, and investment. Globalization is a complicated phenomenon, influenced by economic, technological, political, and social aspects, continuing to evolve and impact the media economy. With this overview of globalization, our examination in this chapter turns to how globalization relates to the media economy.

GLOBALIZATION AND THE MEDIA INDUSTRIES

Why does a media company engage in globalization? There can be many reasons for "going global," but most activity is driven by very simple business decisions. Most companies seek to move beyond their domestic borders to expand and grow their market share—a basic tenet of economic theory, discussed in Chapter 3, that a firm seeks to maximize its value for its owners and shareholders. The domestic markets in many countries are both fully developed and saturated. There is little room to expand market share except on an incremental basis (Anderson, 2006). More opportunities for business growth and expansion may be found outside domestic borders.

The unique nature of media products allows for many possibilities for expansion of market share by media companies. Media products are public goods, and they are unique in that they can be used over and over again. Content can be recycled to new and younger audiences on a constantly evolving basis. Media products do have a high production cost, primarily owing to the union and craft guild wages required for writers, directors, producers, and talent—yet their reproduction costs are marginal, especially in a digital environment where the content can exist solely as a digital file.

It is impossible to forecast demand for media products; there is a high degree of uncertainty that exists in the development and marketing of content. Few efforts will result in a franchise like Harry Potter or Spider-Man, and combined production and marketing costs (especially for film) add to the stress factor. It is also difficult to measure the true value of media products, because they are highly instrumental and used and consumed in different ways. Following the theory of the long tail (Anderson, 2006), we also know that media products are capable of adding incremental value over time. The products have value to audiences, but also to advertisers. In short, globalization of media carries a lot of potential, but also a great deal of risk.

Television and Film Products

Media products like movies and television programs can easily be distributed to other countries with native language added as sub-titles or dubbed in. Hollywood films became a staple of TV programming in many countries as television was adopted around the globe, because movies could be acquired cheaply and would provide several hours of content. Eventually, television series would be offered to the international marketplace for acquisition.

For content creators and distributors, the international marketplace meant the opportunities for expanded revenues were greatly multiplied. A film or television series could generate even more revenues beyond domestic borders without adding any costs to the actual production process. And, with the ability to reuse media content products, the content can be repackaged and resold over and over again to new clients.

Content creators and distributors recognized early the importance of the international marketplace and the vast opportunity to grow additional revenues. But there were caveats. Not all products could be sold everywhere owing to differences in local culture and customs. For example, television situation comedies are often challenging to market internationally because scripts tend to be specific to local culture and customs. *Seinfeld*, one of the most popular comedies in America, was not an international hit because of the program's unique context. In short, people in other countries didn't understand the program. In contrast, *Friends*, originally adapted from a British comedy, was a monster hit globally, and can still be seen in many countries.

While comedy can be challenging to export, two types of content are universally understood around the globe: sex and violence. The international marketplace contains a lot of content built around sex and/or violence. For example, the most widely distributed television program in history was *Baywatch*, a program known for beautiful lifeguards in sexy swimwear set in Southern California. At its height, Baywatch was seen in 148 countries and translated into 44 different languages (*Ratings winners*, n.d.). In terms of violence, TV franchises built around violent crimes like *CSI* and *Law and Order* remain popular in the international market.

The United States is the largest exporter of television programming around the globe, although the U.S. imports very little programming (Cooper-Chen, 2005). Almost all of the imported TV programming comes from Great Britain (Griffin, 2005). Mexico, home of the conglomerate Grupo Televisa, exports a great deal of

Table 7.1 All-Time Worldwide Box Office Receipts (as of July 1, 2009)

RANKING	FILM	GLOBAL BOX OFFICE
1.	*Titanic* (1997)	$1,835,300,000
2.	*The Lord of the Rings: The Return of the King* (2003)	$1,129,219,252
3.	*Pirates of the Caribbean: Dead Man's Chest* (2006)	$1,060,332,628
4.	*The Dark Knight* (2008)	$1,001,921,825
5.	*Harry Potter and the Sorcerer's Stone* (2001)	$968,657,891
6.	*Pirates of the Caribbean: At World's End* (2007)	$958,404,152
7.	*Harry Potter and the Order of the Phoenix* (2007)	$937,000,866
8.	*Star Wars: Episode I—The Phantom Menace* (1999)	$922,379,000
9.	*The Lord of the Rings: The Two Towers* (2002)	$921,600,000
10.	*Jurassic Park* (1993)	$919,700,000

Source: *All-time worldwide box office* (n.d.).

programming (primarily novellas and football [soccer] matches) to Spanish-speaking countries (Gutierrez, 2009). Brazil, the home of Globo TV, is actually the largest exporter of novellas around the world, according to Silva (2005).

In terms of film, the United States is also the top film exporter in the world, with the global film marketplace dominated entirely by Hollywood films produced and distributed by American-based companies. It should be noted that the U.S. is the top producer of box office receipts, but not the top producer of *total* films. India holds that distinction, as "Bollywood" (the name for Indian cinema) produces more films on an annual basis than the United States, and has for many years. A good source for tracking box office sales of global films is the Internet Movie Database (www.imdb.com), which is updated on a regular basis. Table 7.1 lists the top ten films in terms of global box office receipts. Note the listing does not include revenues from video rentals and sales, television rights, or other revenues.

GLOBAL STRATEGIES

There is a variety of possible strategies employed by media-based companies with a desire to participate in the global market. Sanchez-Tabernero (2006) provides one analysis of global strategies, focusing on four distinct areas: 1) the creation of national and international media products; 2) scale economies and diversification; 3) seeking opportunities and attractive markets; and 4) moving towards internationalization in a series of stages. While these first three areas have been discussed in other chapters of the book, the fourth area deserves a bit more elaboration.

Sanchez-Tabernero (2006) identifies four stages of pursuing a globalization strategy, all designed to develop a competitive advantage over other competitors. These areas are highlighted below:

- *Stage One—Building a strong domestic position.* The author discusses three different possibilities: building a presence as a strong national company (e.g., Comcast); highly specialized companies that are leaders in a specific sector (e.g., Bertelsmann as in book publishing); and regional groups that acquire or develop media in the capital city of a nation and other large urban areas (e.g., New York Times Company).
- *Stage Two—Initial presence in international arena.* In this stage the company moves outside of domestic borders, either making a small entry into a single country or pursuing a larger strategy. Content products may simply be repackaged or modified, or new content may be created for entry into the new market. Relationships with foreign partners are essential to eliminating unnecessary risk and providing contacts and an understanding of the local culture. An example is Telefonica, which is based in Spain but has broadened its reach in many Latin American countries.
- *Stage Three—Consolidating an international presence.* The author points out that when exports make up at least 25% of a company's business it has successfully consolidated its presence as an international company. New goals are refined, and entry into other countries is common. Organizational structures begin to evolve, with locations in other countries. Examples of companies that have passed through this stage include Walt Disney and Sony.
- *Stage Four—Formation of transnational groups.* As the organization continues to expand and evolve, with more profits coming from many different international sectors, companies become transnational in nature. At the global level, this has led to the formation of what Gershon (2005) calls transnational media companies, the focus of the next section.

TRANSNATIONAL MEDIA COMPANIES

Most of the media globalization activities that take place around the globe are driven by large media conglomerates, also called transnational media corporations (TRMCs). Gershon (2005, p. 17) describes the transnational media corporation as an entity with "overseas operations in two or more countries" where "strategic decision making and the allocation of resources are predicated on economic goals and efficiencies with little regard to national boundaries" and the "principle commodity being sold is information and entertainment."

A global oligopoly of these TRMCs dominates the media marketplace, accounting for a large share of the revenues generated from the sale of media content products and advertising. Most of these firms started owning just a single business operation, and grew by acquisition and mergers. Table 7.2 lists the major TRMCs as of mid-2009.

Let's take a closer look at these TRMCs in terms of how these companies are structured and managed. This information is presented in Table 7.3.

The officer column refers to the number of corporate officers in the company. Directors refer to the number making up the board of directors for the company. Employees refer to global employees. As seen in Table 7.3, the number of officers and directors for these companies averages around ten officers (excluding Bertelsmann) and 14 directors. The size of the employee base varies, with conglomerates like General Electric (parent of NBC Universal) and Sony employing a large manufacturing base. Chapter 11 offers a more detailed look at labor and employment in the media.

To understand the importance of globalization to these TRMCs, Table 7.4 compares the financial performance of these companies by

Table 7.2 Major Transnational Media Corporations (2009)

COMPANY	HEADQUARTERS	CORE HOLDINGS
CBS	USA	TV networks and stations, radio.
NBC Universal	USA	TV networks, studios, cable channels.
News Corporation	USA	TV networks, studios, newspapers.
Time Warner	USA	Studios, TV programming, publishing.
Viacom	USA	Cable channels, pay cable, publishing.
Walt Disney	USA	Studios, theme parks, TV networks.
Sony	Japan	Electronics, studios, video game consoles.
Bertelsmann AG	Germany	Book and magazine publishing, TV programs.

Source: Compiled by the author from company reports and websites.

Table 7.3   TRMC Structure (as of July 2009)

COMPANY	CEO	OFFICERS	DIRECTORS	EMPLOYEES
CBS	Les Moonves	14	14	25,920
NBC Universal	Jeff Zucker	19	16	323,000[a]
News Corporation	Rupert Murdoch	13	17	64,000
Time Warner	Jeffrey L. Bewkes	7	10	87,000
Viacom	Philippe Dauman	12	11	11,500
Walt Disney	Robert Iger	17	12	150,000
Sony	Howard Stringer	8	15	171,300
Bertelsmann AG	Hartmut Ostrowski	35	15	106,083

a Refers to total employees for General Electric, parent company of NBC Universal.

Source: Compiled by the author from company reports and websites.

Table 7.4   Financial Performance of TRMCs, 2008

COMPANY	2008 REVENUE (MILLIONS USD)	GLOBAL REVENUE (MILLIONS USD)	GLOBAL REVENUE AS A PERCENTAGE OF TOTAL REVENUE
CBS	13,950	2,246	16%
NBC Universal	16,969	N/A	N/A
News Corporation	32,996	9,808*	30%
Time Warner	46,984	N/A	N/A
Viacom	14,625	4,241	29%
Walt Disney	37,843	9,337*	25%
Sony	79,808	60,654	76%
Bertelsmann AG	22,565	14,370	64%

Notes: Sony figures converted to dollars from Japanese yen. Sony is a publicly held company. Bertelsmann figures converted to dollars from euros. Bertelsmann is a privately held firm. For both Sony and Bertelsmann, global revenue is based on revenues outside of Japan and Germany respectively.

* Estimated figure based on company filings.

Source: Compiled by author from corporate websites and company filings.

breaking down their revenues in the international arena, using data that is publicly available. Some interesting observations can be made from the data presented in Table 7.4.

For TRMCs based in the U.S., global revenue in 2008 ranged from a low of 16% for CBS to as much as 30% for News Corporation. However, for those outside of the U.S. the importance of global revenues is even greater; Sony derived 76% of its revenues outside of Japan, while

Bertelsmann garnered 64% of its revenues outside of Germany. For both of these companies, revenues from the United States and Europe accounted for the bulk of each company's global income.

Transnational media companies, or large media conglomerates, continue to dominate the media economy in the 21st century. The sheer financial power and reach of these companies give them a strong competitive position compared to the case of those countries whose indigenous media firms are pursuing a national or local strategy. We can also expect further evolution of companies identified as transnational media companies. As this book was going to press, there was a pending merger in which Comcast Corporation would acquire 51% of the assets of NBC Universal, and General Electric would hold the other 49% with provisions to eventually sell its entire stake. At what point does a company like Google deserve to be listed as a transnational media company, given the strength of its holdings in the Internet sector? If history is any guide to the future, we know that the composition of TRMCs changes over time, primarily through merger and acquisition.

SUMMARY

This chapter introduces and discusses globalization as a force impacting the media economy. "Globalization" is a multi-faceted term, whose meanings vary depending on the context in which the subject is examined. While globalization has existed for centuries, the topic has taken on much greater interest and influence since the 1970s, when a series of events (the 1974 oil crisis, the financial crisis of the 1980s, the fall of the Berlin Wall in 1989, the creation of the World Trade Organization in 1995) demonstrated how the globe is connected.

There are positive and negative aspects connected with globalization. In terms of positives, globalization strengthens competition, increases productivity, and spurs innovation. In terms of negatives, globalization is cited as creating global political institutions and global economic institutions driven by money and power. From a media perspective, globalization is criticized for creating a homogeneous global culture, ignoring the values and culture of domestic countries.

Globalization was also discussed in terms of regional trade blocs and agreements, which drive further efforts at internationalization. The WTO estimates there were over 120 trade blocs in existence as of 2009, with many countries part of multiple trade groups. The three largest trade blocs are found in North America (NAFTA), Europe (the European Union), and Asia (Asia-Pacific Economic Cooperation or APEC).

Next, the chapter examined globalization and the media industries, detailing why media-related firms seek to enter the international market. Also discussed in this section was the unique nature of television and film products, and examples from different regions of the world were considered.

Global strategies were also introduced following insights from Sanchez-Tabernero (2006). The four stages of developing an international strategy, leading to the creation of large conglomerates, also known as transnational media corporations (TRMCs), were reviewed. Data on the world's eight largest TRMCs were presented in terms of location, core holdings, structure, and financial performance.

Globalization remains a driver of the media economy, and will continue to evolve as a force, in part because of the challenges in trying to regulate internationalization of the media industries (see Chakravartty & Sarikakis, 2006). Globalization offers both promises and pitfalls for companies seeking to compete at an international level.

DISCUSSION QUESTIONS

1. Globalization is a key force impacting the media industries. How do you feel about globalization? Do you see it as a positive force or a negative force? Why?

2. What are some of the reasons that firms seek to enter a global marketplace? What can be gained by globalization?

3. One strategy for entering the global marketplace is to do so in stages. What can be gained by proceeding in stages? How does it limit risk?

4. At present the global media marketplace is dominated by eight major TRMCs. Do you see any other companies emerging to compete with these TRMCs? If so, which companies and why?

5. Do you think globalization will continue to be a key force driving the media economy in the 21st century? Why or why not?

CHAPTER 8

Regulation and the Media Economy

In this chapter you will learn:

- how a country's political philosophy influences the type of regulation found in the nation;
- how governments use regulation to influence markets;
- the different levels of policy where regulation occurs;
- where and how regulation is used across the media economy.

Regulation is another external factor that impacts the media economy. Regulation is a given with any government; laws and policies are used to address a number of national interests and social policy goals. Regulation in most countries has its foundations in a maxim known as "the rule of law," which has its origins in ancient Greece through the writings of Plato and Aristotle around 360 BC. The Magna Carta, which was signed by England's King John in 1215, became a critical document influencing the development of common laws, with principles embodied in many countries' legal documents, such as the U.S. Constitution, adopted in 1787.

Regulation covers many facets of society and functions at different levels, as does the media economy. Governments use regulation to serve many roles, such as establish laws, levy taxation, establish a military and national defense, meet social policy goals, and for the purposes of this chapter regulate markets as needed to protect the interests of the people and society as a whole. Needless to say, businesses—especially those operating in a capitalistic environment such as a mixed market— prefer to have as little governmental regulation as possible. Regulation in a general sense can limit the profit potential of a business as well as overall market share.

Regulation of the media industries is challenging for government, in part because of digital technology and the fact that markets are so intertwined and interdependent (Cherry, 2006). In this chapter, regulation is examined in the following ways. First, we examine the role of government and regulation by looking at the philosophical orientation of the respective government, followed by the different levels on which regulation occurs. Next, we will look at various categories of regulatory policy that are inherent in most governments around the globe. Finally, we will look at the impact of regulation on the media economy, using examples from actual policy actions around the globe.

REGULATION AND GOVERNMENT

Earlier in this text, you were introduced to the three types of economies and their philosophies: the command economy, the market economy, and the mixed economy. Recall that in reality the market economy is more of an ideal than an established system; therefore, in terms of regulatory policy the mixed economy dominates much of the globe, but the command economy can still be found in certain countries that are not orientated towards a democracy.

In a command economy, exemplified by nations like North Korea, Cuba, and Iran, the government controls virtually all aspects of commerce and society. In the case of media policy, the government either owns or controls the media, and private ownership is not allowed. Countries such as Russia and China have adopted capitalistic ideals by allowing foreign companies to enter the countries, but neither country has given up control of its media operations, meaning all of the dominant media are either state-owned or state-controlled.

Thus, most of the world operates with a mixed economy, meaning that there is a combination of a market economy orientation along with a regulatory policy. In these countries, regulatory decisions are used to provide economic policies, influence markets, and prevent anti-competitive practices and monopolistic behavior, among other topics.

Where regulation establishes laws, governments also can make changes in existing policies via three other tools: deregulation, liberalization, and privatization. A brief explanation of each of these regulatory efforts is described below.

In deregulation, a law or policy is removed or rescinded. The law or policy may have become outdated or obsolete, or removed to eliminate bureaucracy. Some examples of media deregulation include the removal of requirements for a radio operator (the personality or "DJ") to have a license, and the elimination of the "Fairness Doctrine" which required broadcasters to seek out opposing views on issues.

Liberalization occurs when a government "liberalizes" a law or policy, allowing more latitude than under prior regulation. For example, in the U.S. the Congress has liberalized ownership limits of radio stations over the years. When a law on ownership limits was initially established, no company or individual could own more than seven AM or seven FM radio stations. These numbers changed several times up until the 1996 Telecommunications Act was passed, allowing for unlimited national ownership, but imposing local ownership caps in each market depending on the size of the market.

In privatization, the government allows a private enterprise to take over what used to be under government control and oversight. Many European governments used to have an agency or "ministry" charged with control of postal services, telecommunications, and telegraph, known as "PTTs" (Steinfield, Bauer, & Caby, 1994) Over time, governments realized they could not manage such entities efficiently and meet all of their other demands, and thus allowed private enterprise to take over these services and operate for a profit.

Government regulations are designed for many similar purposes across countries, and governments also use the tools of deregulation, liberalization, and privatization to make adjustments to establishing law and policy. The following list represents a few of the more common areas where governments take regulatory action for their citizens:

- *Taxation.* All governments levy taxes on both individuals and businesses. Taxes provide the revenues to provide services and to pay for government projects.
- *Defense.* Many governments use taxes to establish a military force to provide for defense against external threats as well as internal conflicts.
- *Labor and personnel.* Most governments establish laws regarding labor and minimum wages, and other laws designed to protect workers.
- *Civil/criminal code.* All governments establish their own codes regarding civil and criminal offenses.
- *Social services.* Governments provide aid and resources ranging from such areas as health care for uninsured citizens to programs like social security, Medicare, and Medicaid.
- *Financial markets.* Governments regulate their financial markets in many ways, such as enforcing accounting standards, requiring

financial statements, establishing interest rates, and engaging in trade and commerce with other countries.

• *Competition and anti-competitive policies.* Most democratic governments establish laws to encourage competition and prevent anti-competitive or monopolistic practices.

This is just a brief listing of examples of areas where governments establish regulatory policy. But where does this regulation actually take place? Regulation ultimately occurs at different levels in most governments, as addressed in the next section.

LEVELS OF POLICY AND REGULATION

Many countries around the globe operate with at least three levels of regulatory policy; these include the national or federal level (as identified in the United States and a host of other countries), the state level, and the local level. Generally speaking, national laws and regulatory policy supersede both the state and the local laws, while state policies supersede local laws. However, situations vary from country to country.

Using the United States as an example, at the national or federal level regulatory policy is the responsibility of the legislative branch of government, manifested by the Congress, which is made up of officials elected by the people to serve in the Senate and House of Representatives. Laws passed by Congress need final approval by the President of the United States, representing the executive branch of government. The President can veto (deny) a law (usually presented as a bill), but Congress has the power to override the President's "nay" vote if two-thirds of Congress vote in favor of such action. This system provides one example of a "checks and balances" process inherent in many democratic governments, to prevent one branch of government from dominating policy decisions.

The system is similar at the state level. States have their own legislative body elected by the people; often these institutions mimic the federal level by having a state house of representatives and a state senate. State laws must be signed into approval by the governor of the state or, like the President, the governor can veto a pending bill, but their decisions can also be overridden with enough votes. States regulate in conjunction with the federal government, but apply law and policy to unique characteristics of each state.

The local level can include regulations at a county or township level, usually having to do with taxation or other unique aspects of local county government, which has responsibility for a geographical region within a state. There are typically several cities or towns within a county that also have their own local regulatory body, usually a city council or board that deals purely with policy decisions, along with the top locally elected official, often known as a mayor.

While this discussion covers the basic organization of most regulatory systems, there are a number of other important areas where regulatory action takes place or influences regulatory action. These areas are discussed in the next section of the chapter.

OTHER CATEGORIES OF REGULATORY ACTION AND INFLUENCE

The Judicial System

The judicial branch or court system represents another important aspect of regulatory policy in any country. In the United States, the judicial branch consists of the Supreme Court (the highest court in the land) and other federal and district courts. States also have similar judicial systems. At the local level there are entities like municipal courts and criminal courts to address cases unique to that level of government.

It is the function of the court system to select and deliberate cases, levy judgments and fines, and provide opinions and decisions. Many times legal cases represent challenges to existing laws and policy. The courts are often asked to determine if the laws are constitutional. Cases can sometimes take years to work through the legal system, with the possibility of appeals at all levels except at the Supreme Court.

Regulatory Agencies

In addition to the various branches and levels, regulatory agencies are created by governments to assist with the regulatory process, usually to focus on specific areas of policy decision-making. Regulatory agencies function at all levels of government, and work with lawmakers to establish rules and laws.

In terms of regulating the media economy, numerous regulatory agencies influence policy. At the federal level in the U.S. the most important regulatory agency is the Federal Communications Commission (FCC), which is charged by Congress with the oversight of both wired and wireless communications. The FCC oversees a number of key areas of media policy covering the broadcast, cable, satellite, and telecommunications industries, as well as some aspects of the Internet— most notably access issues. The FCC is charged with such areas of policy as establishing ownership limits and licensing requirements for broadcasters, and providing universal service for telephone customers.

The Federal Trade Commission (FTC) is another key regulatory agency operating at the federal level in the U.S. One of the key responsibilities of the FTC is oversight of advertising, including investigations regarding false or deceptive advertising and unlawful trade practices.

At the state level, regulatory agencies work in conjunction with federal agencies to influence policy. For example, many states have utility commissions or agencies that oversee access to public utilities and in some cases rate regulation. There are also state agencies that deal with specific industries like insurance, medical care, and motor vehicles.

Regulatory agencies at the local level are more limited in scope, but still serve important roles. These may be appointed boards or committees charged with specific tasks and functions, such as appraisal boards which determine property tax rates. Boards of education, hospital boards, and many other agencies work together with state officials to provide services and assistance at the local level.

Self-Regulation and Industry Associations

Most industries attempt to limit undue governmental regulation by engaging in self-regulation. This is particularly evident in the media economy, where content can be accessed widely from a number of platforms. For the most part, media companies are conservative regarding their programming and content; they do not want to offend audiences (consumers) or advertisers with controversial material that could raise public concern and scrutiny. The infamous "wardrobe malfunction" in the 2004 Super Bowl halftime broadcast to an international audience set off a storm of controversy over indecent material and responsibility that is still being sorted out in the court system years later. Companies have found that self-regulation is an ongoing process that constantly raises questions regarding ethics and standards of what it is appropriate to program, broadcast, or publish.

In particular to media, industry associations have formed over the years to help lobby and influence policymakers on the nuances of their respective industries. Organizations like the National Association of Broadcasters (NAB), the National Cable and Telecommunications Association, the Motion Picture Association of America, and the Recording Industry Association of America (RIAA) are just a few of the media trade associations that are primarily lobbying groups.

It is not uncommon for trade associations to battle one another over legislation, especially with economic issues. An example is the ongoing conflict between the RIAA (representing record companies and artists) and the NAB (representing the radio industry) regarding the possible establishment of a performance rights fee or tax (depending on the viewpoint) on the radio industry. To simplify the conflict, the RIAA wants legislation to provide more revenues to artists for their performances, while the radio industry argues they promote artists and their careers with free airplay, and any legislation would take millions of dollars from their declining revenues. In this case, both associations are lobbying Congress—one to create a new law, the other to try to prevent it from happening.

Citizen Groups, Critics, and Media Literacy

In any democracy, the will of the people is manifested through many rights, such as the right to vote in the election process. But there are many other ways "the people" or ordinary citizens can influence regulatory processes aside from electing officials to office.

One way is through citizen groups, which are simply organizations where members share common interests and concerns. They may also provide a lobbying function to influence laws. Some examples of citizen groups include the Parent Teacher Association (PTA), the American Association of Retired Persons (AARP), the American Civil Liberties Union (ACLU), Mothers Against Drunk Driving (MADD), and the National Rifle Association (NRA). Specific to the media industries are groups like Action for Children's Television (ACT), Fairness and Accuracy in Reporting (FAIR), and the Media Research Center (MRC), to name just a few.

There are numerous media critics who help educate the public about media organizations and content. Many newspapers used to employ media critics, but falling demand for newspapers along with budget cuts eliminated many of these positions. A number of critics simply moved to the Internet, setting up their own blogs and web pages. Critics still maintain a place in serving a watchdog role in regard to the media.

There are many organizations and groups committed to the subject of media literacy, designed to educate and increase public knowledge about the media industries, especially among families with small children. Media literacy groups also have a role in influencing regulation through their activities and membership.

As seen in this section of the chapter, there are a number of influences on policies for the media economy, ranging from regulatory agencies to self-regulating efforts and citizen groups. Next we will look at different categories of media policy from around the globe.

REGULATION AND THE MEDIA ECONOMY

In this section of the chapter our focus is on specific categories of media regulation and policy enacted by governments. Examples from around the world are offered as these topics are discussed to illustrate how regulatory policy varies from nation to nation.

Content Regulation

In most nations functioning with a mixed economy, the regulation of media content is limited to just a few areas, as many countries embody the idea of free speech or free expression. An exception is those countries operating under a command philosophy, which tend to deny free expression to publishers and broadcasters, as these entities are typically government-controlled. Here are some of the primary areas where content regulation exists in a mixed economy:

- *Content for children.* Many countries have adopted specific policies regarding content for children, especially in the television sector. The goal is to offer programming that has educational value and limits the amount of advertising. In the United States, television stations are required to broadcast three hours of educational programming each week. Other nations with specific policies concerning media content targeting children include the United Kingdom, Sweden, and Norway.
- *Sex and violence.* Content with sexual content and dialogue, along with content that features gratuitous violence, is a concern for regulators as well. Different countries have attempted to deal with this through different policies, but cultural norms vary greatly. In the United States, broadcasters generally avoid any nudity, whereas in many European nations nudity is allowed. Violence is more prevalent on TV in the U.S. and minimized in Europe. The United States and some other nations have developed voluntary ratings systems to warn families about content that may contain sex and violence.
- *Indecency and obscenity.* Many nations offer guidelines regarding material that is indecent or obscene. Interestingly, in the U.S., indecency is protected by the First Amendment, as long as it is used in the time period known as the "safe harbor" (10:00 p.m. to 6:00 a.m.), when children are not as likely to be watching television. Obscenity on the other hand is material that typically lacks any sort of "literary, artistic, political, or scientific value" (the LAPS test), using the U.S. Supreme Court's

definition of obscenity. Obscenity violations in many countries carry significant fines and even prison sentences for those found guilty.

- *Film boards and commissions.* Some countries still have operating film boards and commissions to screen motion pictures to determine if they are acceptable to their citizens. At one time there were many film boards operating in the U.S., but most have been dissolved. With content accessible on DVD and through the Internet, it became challenging if not impossible to regulate, and "protect" citizens from certain types of content. In the U.S. many theaters engage in self-regulation and refuse to show films that have been designated as "NC-17" (no children under 17); as a result, only a handful of films have received such a rating since the label was created.

Ownership and Control of Media

Many countries have specific guidelines involving both the ownership and the control of media. Here are some examples of ownership and control policies:

- *Licensing.* In order to operate a broadcast station or multichannel enterprise like a cable, satellite, or IPTV system, applicants must obtain a license or a franchise from the government. To obtain a license, citizenship is a requirement, along with detailed financial qualifications and other requirements. Licenses are normally for a specific time period, and subject to renewal. Likewise, when media outlets are sold, there is usually a process involved to transfer control of a license to the new owners to ensure they meet all regulatory requirements.
- *Ownership limits.* A number of countries establish limits on the number of media outlets (radio, TV stations, etc.) one individual or company may own. This is to ensure ownership diversity as well as diversity of expression. However, the rise of global media conglomerates and their many holdings are an area of concern for policymakers and media activists (see Bagdikian, 2004; McChesney, 2007).
- *Foreign investment.* Many nations limit foreign ownership and investment in local media to a non-controlling percentage, usually no more than 25–30%. This is to ensure that majority control remains domiciled in the country of license. A sample of

the many countries that limit foreign ownership of the media include the United States, France, Germany, Mexico, Brazil, Chile, and Ecuador.

- *Minority ownership and participation in media.* Some nations have attempted to ensure minority ownership of media outlets. In this sense, minorities typically represent indigenous or underserved populations. Not all nations have been successful with such policies. Minority ownership in the United States is extremely limited, despite several policy attempts and government programs to help qualified minorities obtain licenses. In a number of Latin American countries (e.g., Bolivia, Brazil, Colombia, Venezuela, Ecuador) the ruling Whites have dominated media ownership for decades, squeezing out the indigenous native populations.

- *Subsidies and taxes.* Subsidies refer to government support of the media. Many of the Scandinavian countries (e.g., Norway, Sweden, and Finland) have a history of providing press subsidies. Many nations also subsidize their public broadcast stations. The United Kingdom is one of a few countries that require a license fee from individual households, which supports the British Broadcasting Corporation (BBC). As of 2009 the monthly fee was just under £12 a month (*Spending your licence fee*, n.d.) or about $20. The license fee provides the main financial support for the BBC, which enables the many services to be provided commercial-free. Political parties also have a history of subsidizing media operations, mostly in the area of publishing newspapers.

Censorship

Censorship occurs when speech or information is suppressed. While generally frowned upon by democratic governments, censorship still exists in many parts of the world and can influence the economic activity of the media in countries that exercise censorship. Several nations provide examples of censorship activity in the 21st century. Here are a few examples:

- *Venezuela.* President Hugo Chavez has nationalized many media outlets, including several key television stations and hundreds of radio stations in an effort to quash opposition and promote his socialistic views (see Chavez's bugbear, 2009; Switched off, 2009).

- *Argentina.* President Cristina Kirchner has created new laws to move more control of the media under the executive branch of her government, in order to effectively shut down much of the free press (O'Grady, 2009). Kirchner has openly targeted the Clarin Group for their criticism, to the point that the President wants to force a breakup of the company (Bad news for some, 2009).
- *Iran.* Iran's Revolutionary Guard Corps, already a dominant military and political force in the country, intends to open a news agency in the spring of 2010 that many believe will ultimately control the flow of information from Iran (Fassihi, 2009).
- *Saudi Arabia, Iran, China, Myanmar, Thailand, Malaysia, Vietnam.* All of these Southeast Asia nations are known to actively filter Internet content flowing in and out of the country in order to control political opposition and criticism (Hookway, 2009). Many of these countries also have been known to intimidate local journalists and bloggers to try to influence their online discussions.

Advertising

Advertising is the major category of financial support in most countries of the world, and in most nations some regulatory policies exist which affect advertising or the advertising of certain types of products. Here are a few examples of policies involving advertising:

- *Limits on advertising.* Most commonly found in broadcasting, many nations have limits regarding how many minutes per hour can be devoted to advertising. Abuse of these limits can result in fines or loss of the right to broadcast.
- *Content restrictions.* Some nations prohibit certain products from being advertised, typically on radio and television. Tobacco is one product. The United States banned tobacco advertising in 1971; the United Kingdom also bans tobacco advertising on billboards and at sporting events. London and Sao Paulo are two large cities that have regulations regarding outdoor displays.
- *Advertising targeting children.* Nations often set limits on the amount and types of advertising that can be placed in programming geared towards children. Sweden and Norway do not even allow advertising targeted to children.
- *False claims.* Advertising that features false claims or inaccurate

information is subject to fines and litigation in many countries. The problem is that many of these advertisements often "run" before the false claims are identified.

Intellectual Property

The World Intellectual Property Organization (WIPO) declares intellectual property "refers broadly to the creations of the human mind. Intellectual property rights protect the interests of creators by giving them property rights over their creations" (WIPO, 2009). Intellectual property in this sense includes such areas as literary and artistic works, broadcast and other performances, patents and trademarks, and scientific works (Gantchev, 2008). Intellectual property consists of two main categories: industrial property and copyright. In this chapter, our focus is on copyright, as this area protects much of the content generated in the media economy.

Copyright protection has been hampered by the development of digital technology and the file-sharing that takes place on the Internet. Numerous copyright violations take place every day in the media economy, despite the best efforts of content creators and distributors to limit such activity. Billions of music files are downloaded and transferred every day around the world. The author has experienced first-hand the sale of pirate CDs and DVDs in Russia and China, and illegal sales happen all over the world, robbing content creators of millions of dollars in sales.

Many governments have copyright laws, and do their best to enforce them, but it is a huge challenge in a digital world where copy-protection protocols can usually be broken by a "hacker" and where peer-to-peer file-sharing remains a reality, despite efforts to close down illegal operations like Kazaa, Morpheus, and the original Napster.

Education is one of the best ways to minimize the impact of copyright violation and abuse of intellectual property. Students, who often are among the worst offenders, need to understand how illegal copying and file-sharing affect the livelihood of the various industries forming the media economy. Education, government efforts, and legal action (as done in the recording industry) are the only ways to limit copyright infringement and protection of intellectual property.

Internet Neutrality and Access

A growing issue in the United States and other nations concerns the idea of Internet or "net" neutrality. At the heart of this issue is the idea of free and open access—with no restrictions on content, platforms, or the kinds of equipment that may be used to connect to the Internet. Further, the principle of net neutrality means that any user should be able to connect with any other user or access point without facing delays or having to pay for higher rates of service.

The debate over net neutrality is complex and multi-faceted. Proponents of net neutrality like Google and Yahoo!, to name just two, argue that broadband providers (e.g., telecommunications and cable television companies) want to impose a tiered service model on users. A tiered model could mean heavier users would pay more for access than lighter users, and it could also involve higher rates at peak times of the day. Another concern is that telcos and cable providers will impose limits that will slow certain types of content (such as peer-to-peer sharing). Telco and cable providers argue that without some discrimination the overall quality of service will erode.

Here is a review of how some nations are addressing the debate on net neutrality:

- In the U.S., the FCC under the Obama administration has made net neutrality a priority. Generally speaking the U.S. supports net neutrality. But broadband carriers continue to challenge the principle and to seek some regulatory guidelines from the government.
- The Canadian government is debating net neutrality. While generally open on the concept, Canada has had problems with some Internet service providers curtailing the speed of the network as well as blocking websites critical of the local ISPs.
- The European Union continues debating net neutrality, and hopes to pass a new law supporting the concept by summer 2010. Italy already has passed some legislation ensuring open access to the Internet.
- In Asia, Japan has adopted network neutrality, as has South Korea. But China represents a huge challenge, with the country blocking most Internet traffic critical of the government.
- Broadband in Latin America as a region is modest, except in Chile, and the situation in Mexico is improving. Network neutrality has not been a topic of debate in the region owing to the lower broadband penetration.

SUMMARY

This chapter has examined the role of regulation in the media economy. The chapter began with a broad discussion of how regulation is used to establish policy in the different types of economies (command, market, mixed) found around the globe. Concepts such as deregulation, liberalization, and privatization were defined, along with a discussion of some of the similar areas that governments establish laws and policies, such as taxation, defense, and labor and personnel.

Policy and regulation also occur at different levels of government, ranging from the national or federal level to the state and local. Many governments operate with an executive, legislative, and judicial system at both federal and state levels.

The chapter discussed other influences on policy particular to the media economy, such as regulatory agencies, industry or self-regulation, citizen groups, and media critics.

Next, specific categories of media regulation and policy were examined broadly, using examples of actual media policy from around the globe. Among the areas discussed in this section were content regulation, ownership and control of the media, censorship, advertising, protection of intellectual property, and Internet or "net" neutrality and open access.

Regulation is a constantly evolving force that impacts all areas of business and society. In regard to the media economy, regulation is used in many different ways both to influence and to regulate markets and economic activity. An understanding of regulation and the regulatory process is critical in our understanding of how the media economy functions. In the next chapter, the focus shifts to another key influence on the media economy, as we examine the social and consumer impact on the media industries.

DISCUSSION QUESTIONS

1. Regulation is used in many different ways to influence markets and economic activity. Why is it necessary for governments to be involved in regulation?
2. Many countries utilize three branches of government (executive, legislative, and judicial) in addition to regulatory agencies to enact rules and laws to influence markets. But one common practice for business and industry is self-regulation. What is self-regulation, and what role does it play in the regulatory process?
3. A lot of media regulation is geared towards areas such as content (protecting children) and ownership. Why are these two areas so important, and how do they differ around the globe?
4. Censorship is generally frowned upon in countries operating

with a mixed economy. What is censorship, and why do some governments openly engage in censorship involving the media industries?

5. The Internet has raised a number of legal issues since its development. One hot issue in the 21st century is that of net neutrality. What is net neutrality, and what are the two main opposing views on the topic?

CHAPTER 9

Social Aspects of the Media Economy

In this chapter you will learn:

- the important role consumers play in the media economy;
- differences between mass media and consumer media;
- how culture, gender, life cycle, and ethnicity affect media consumption;
- how consumers allocate time and money to the media economy;
- why consumers expect much of the media content to be available for free.

This chapter centers on yet another important force impacting the media economy, that of the consumer. The consumer is constantly changing and evolving, owing to shifts in demographics and population as well as in regard to tastes and preferences. The consumer is the ultimate goal in the media economy for firms and advertisers. Firms create content to attract consumers; advertisers purchase time and space in order to access these consumers. Consumers contribute significantly to a nation's GDP; in the United States, it is estimated that consumer spending accounts for as much as 70% of America's GDP (*Facts on policy,* 2006).

This chapter uses the term "social aspects" to refer to consumers and their impact on the media economy. "Social aspects" is a broad label but is used purposely here to recognize the wide influence of consumers at all levels of the media economy. In this sense, social aspects represent significant forces impacting the media economy through their individual and aggregate allocation of how much time the consumer spends on media products, and how much money the consumer spends on media products.

The chapter first considers the basic role of consumers in the media economy. From there the discussion focuses on: the social and cultural implications involving consumers in the media economy; how gender, life cycle, and ethnicity impact consumer use of the media; an expanded examination of consumer dimensions of time and money, including a detailed analysis of exactly how time and money are spent across the media economy; and how "free" content may evolve in the future.

CONSUMERS IN THE MEDIA ECONOMY

Consumers represent the "prospects" that all media companies and advertising are chasing with their content and messages. Historically, consumers of the media have been identified with the word "mass" because the media industries through the years were able to reach massive amounts of people (e.g., a mass audience) through print publications, broadcasting, movies, and music. The media industries were soon to be identified as "mass media," and many education institutions adopted degree programs and names of departments, colleges, and schools with the term "mass communication."

The terms "mass media" and "mass audience" in one respect implied the consumer was a member of a collective blob; little individuality was expressed or considered, primarily owing to the limited availability of the media. For example, growing up in the 1960s, this author remembers when broadcast television in our local market consisted of three to four channels available via a terrestrial antenna, and the stations broadcast in black and white. By the mid-1970s, cable television had emerged, bringing what would eventually be hundreds of channels into the homes of consumers. Other technologies came into existence, with the result that the heretofore "mass" audience became fragmented, as consumers followed numerous paths to content. This fragmentation was driven by greater choice and access, but it had a devastating impact on the idea of a mass audience.

By the 1980s it was evident that the media industries were evolving, and their ability to attract "mass" audiences would be limited to high-profile, high-event content such as the top sporting events (e.g., Super Bowl), mini-series, and blockbuster movies. In the 1990s, the introduction of the Internet's World Wide Web (along with the original hypertext language that created web pages) ushered in a new era of consumption patterns, as the online world soon began to offer audio and video in a 24/7/365 window, available to anyone with a high-speed connection to the Internet.

In the 21st century, the proliferation of alternative digital platforms

Table 9.1 Comparison of Mass Media to Consumer Media

MASS MEDIA	CONSUMER MEDIA
Control of distribution	Control of access and choice
Linear experience	Non-linear experience
Limited choices	Expanded choices
Limited advertiser options	Many advertiser options
Oligopoly power	Unlimited competitors
Impersonal	Personal and interactive

Source: Author's compilation.

(as discussed in Chapter 5) extended consumer options even further, offering still more choice and flexibility through the use of mobile devices such as laptops with built-in Wi-Fi connectivity, personal digital assistants, and of course smart phones. All of this fragmentation and choice has forced media companies to look at audiences differently. The era of "mass" media is long over. We now function in an era of *consumer* media, where individuals have the choice and flexibility to decide when they consume media, how they consume media, what they consume, and where they consume. A comparison of these two eras is presented in Table 9.1.

CULTURAL IMPLICATIONS

In reality, consumers never truly were a part of a mass, but rather an aggregate of many different groups based on age, gender, ethnicity, language, income, religion, and other characteristics. Consumers also have cultural backgrounds which make them unique. A complete discussion of cultural backgrounds and how they affect media usage and consumption is beyond the scope of this text; here we offer a few simple ideas to help in understanding the complexity of the consumer as a cultural being.

"Culture" is a broad term, encompassing a society's norms, values, beliefs, history, and customs. All of us were born into a cultural system, and our understanding of that system evolved through many different institutions: our immediate family, schools, churches and religious organizations, peers, and organizations we belong to, to name just a few. In our early years, media habits and consumption are usually controlled by family members. This early control influences habits and affects preferences. But, as children grow older and expand their own social circles, they are exposed to new types of media content and mediums. In the heavily fragmented media environment of the 21st century, media use ranges from traditional media forms like books and newspapers to new media content available through digital platforms.

The Impact of Gender on Media Consumption

As John Gray's (1992) popular book clarified how men and women differ on a number of traits and situations, years of audience research clarified how gender impacts media consumption. There are certain genres of programming that primarily appeal to the different sexes. In terms of television genres, women tend to watch more dramas, situation comedies, and talk programs than men. Women enjoy movies that focus on romance and romantic comedies (e.g., "chick" flicks). Men like to watch sports on television, along with situation comedies. In terms of movies, men favor action adventure, science fiction, and horror genres. Men, especially younger males, tend to adopt media-related technology faster than women. Of course, there are always exceptions, but a few of the established gender differences, from a U.S. perspective, are listed in Table 9.2.

Generally speaking, there are differences in regard to adoption of new technologies between men and women. Finally, we also know that advertisers target most of their messages to women, because females make most of the spending decisions in a home.

Table 9.2   Gender Differences and Media Consumption

ITEM	FEMALES	MALES
Content preferences	Dramas, situation comedies, talk programs, romantic comedies.	Sports, action/adventure, science fiction, horror, games.
Advertising	Generally tolerant of advertising; like commercials.	Dislike advertising; see interruptions negatively.
Remote control use	Light users, not likely to change channels as quickly.	Heavy use; will change channels frequently.
Attention span	Longer.	Shorter.

Source: Author's compilation.

Table 9.3 Comparing Life Cycles and Media Habits and Uses

GROUP	DRIVERS	MEDIA USES
Younger audiences (12–24)	Influenced by peers, friends, social networks; family important.	Multitasking; spend more time with new media; most use for remains entertainment.
Adult audiences (25–64)	Concerns for: family and their welfare; career and jobs; economics.	Use both traditional and new media; seek out information and entertainment.
Older audiences (65+)	Health and retirement issues; safety.	Use more traditional media; more news and information.

Source: Author's compilation.

Life Cycle's Impact on Media Consumption

As we move through the life cycle our media habits evolve over time (Dimmick, McCain, & Bolton, 1979). Content that was important to us as children is replaced by other content during the adolescent years. The transition to adulthood brings more changes in regard to media consumption. As people approach middle age and move on to become senior citizens, a further evolution takes place. General differences among life cycles and media use are detailed in Table 9.3.

Ethnicity's Impact on Media Consumption

Ethnicity is also a strong influence on media habits and usage. Research by both the academic and the professional sectors often identifies differences among ethnic segments in regard to content choice, time spent with the media, and technology adoption (see *African-American TV*, 2007; Albarran & Umphrey, 1993, 1994; Arbitron, 2008; *Asian persuasion*, 2008; Umphrey & Albarran, 1993). Table 9.4 illustrates

Table 9.4 Examples of TV Preferences Among U.S. Ethnic Audiences

ANGLOS	AFRICAN AMERICANS	HISPANICS/LATINOS	ASIAN AMERICANS
Reality programs	Reality programs	Novellas	News
Dramas	Sports (mainstream)	Sports (soccer)	Science fiction
Sports (mainstream)	Dramas	News	Movies
Situation comedies	Situation comedies	Music	Music

Source: Adapted from multiple sources by the author.

some of these differences by comparing TV preferences in the U.S. among Anglos, African Americans, Latinos, and Asian Americans.

This comparison of gender, life cycle, and ethnicity on media-related consumption further illustrates one of the key points of this chapter—that the audience is not really a mass entity, but an aggregate of numerous groups aligned along these three variables. There are many other variables that influence media consumption aside from gender, life cycle, and ethnicity—such as income, education level, the presence of children in a household, access to technology, and so on—that are beyond the scope of this discussion. Together, these variables make understanding the individual and their media consumption one of the most interesting and difficult challenges in the media economy.

CONSUMER ALLOCATION OF TIME AND MONEY

Regardless of the gender, age, or ethnicity of the consumer, we can learn much about individual media habits and preferences through the concept of allocation, originally discussed in Chapter 3. In this context, consumer allocation can be thought of as two important decisions: how much *time* is spent with media-related activities, and how much *money* is spent on media-related activities.

Allocation decisions are directly related to supply and demand functions. Applied to individuals, we all face the same constraints on our time—there are only 24 hours in a day, and we engage in many activities during a typical day. In terms of money, most people have a limited supply of funds. Thus, individuals make decisions on how to allocate or spend their supply of money for both necessities (needs) and things we desire (wants).

Allocation decisions can be simple or complex. Everyone approaches allocation decisions differently. Some allocation decisions are made without thinking—like turning on the radio when we are driving in a car, reading a favorite magazine, or watching television during our free time. But these quick decisions were also part of a larger set of decisions. For example, if we subscribe to a multichannel TV service via cable, satellite, or IPTV, we have made a conscious decision to spend so much money per month on a television service. Likewise, if you rent movies each month from a Netflix or Blockbuster you have made an allocation decision. If you purchase or subscribe to a magazine you have made an allocation decision.

Allocation decisions made at the level of the individual and the household are of particular interest to advertisers and media firms, because these decisions ultimately impact advertisers and media companies. Allocation decisions have become even more critical given the ubiquity of media platforms and the availability of a wide variety of media content.

TIME SPENT WITH MEDIA

Our time spent with media content represents an important area of understanding about the media economy. The time we choose to spend with media reflects our individual demand for media products (Albarran & Arrese, 2003). As the media economy has evolved, different patterns of time spent with the media have emerged. Time spent with the media is measured in different ways. For the electronic media, audience ratings collected by Arbitron for radio and Nielsen for television produce trends and patterns of consumption. Movies can be measured by box office ticket sales and rentals and purchases of films. Print products (newspapers, magazines, books) consider the number of copies sold and the amount of time spent reading. Online activities can be identified by measuring which websites and platforms are accessed and the time duration. All of this information provides a picture of time spent with the media.

In the United States, the Census Bureau publishes an annual online compilation of data from various aspects of society known as the *Statistical Abstract* (see http://www.census.gov/compendia/statab/). This document offers insight to the question of how much time is allocated to the media. Table 9.5 offers a partial view of this data, arranged by the number of hours per person per year.

Table 9.5 Estimates of Hours of Media Usage per Person per Year (Age 12-Plus)

CATEGORY	2009	2010	2011
TV (broadcast)	673	673	669
TV (cable/satellite)	1,041	1,055	1,073
Radio (broadcast/satellite)	760	758	751
Newspapers	162	158	154
Internet services	184	184	183
Video games	91	94	100
Magazines	114	112	110
Books	109	109	110
Total media hours	3,569	3,569	3,624

Note: The table does not include estimates for home video and out-of-home media.

Source: Adapted from U.S. Census Bureau (2009).

Table 9.5 illustrates some very interesting trends in terms of media usage. We observe that most areas of "traditional" media (broadcast TV, radio, newspapers, magazines, books) are projected to continue to decline over time, while "newer" media options (cable and satellite TV and video games) are projected to continue an upward trend. Mobile phone use is not even charted yet, and no doubt consumers will allocate more time to smart phones going forward. But perhaps the most interesting trend of all is that the amount of time allocated to total media consumption continues to rise each year, further demonstrating another important aspect of the media economy.

What does a projected 3,569 hours of media usage mean in the life of a typical American citizen, age 18-plus? Let's consider this in context with two other activities that are important to anyone's well-being: work and sleep. Let's assume that the average person 18-plus works a total of 44 weeks a year at an estimated 40 hours of week. This translates to a total of 1,760 hours of work. Let's further propose that the average person averages about seven hours of sleep a day, which translates to a total of 2,555 hours a year. Table 9.6 combines all of this data to resemble how the typical American uses their time.

In a given year each of us has 8,760 hours available for allocating all of our activities, no more and no less. While the information in Table 9.6 is hypothetical (if you work more than 44 weeks a year or sleep less than seven hours a day I understand), it does suggest that individuals spend a large amount of time engaged in media consumption, more so than work or sleep. Of course, we know that a lot of media activity is performed as multitasking; we listen to music while driving or working, as well as watch television while surfing the Internet or reading a magazine. Nevertheless, there is a lot of media consumption taking place at both home and work.

Table 9.6   Estimated Annual Use of Time, 2009 (Adults, 18-Plus)

	TOTAL HOURS	PERCENTAGE OF TIME
Media usage	3,569	41%
Work	1,760	20%
Rest/sleep	2,555	29%
Other time	876	10%

Source: Author's compilation.

CONSUMER SPENDING ON THE MEDIA

Having considered the relationship of how consumers allocate time to the media, the next obvious question to ask is how much do consumers spend on the media and media-related products and activities? McCombs (1972) was one of the first scholars to research this question. The author developed the principle of relative constancy (PRC), and analyzed consumer data at the time that suggested most households spend about 3% of their income on media-related products and services. Later studies both questioned (Wood, 1986) and supported the initial analysis (McCombs & Nolan, 1992). Other researchers examined the PRC in other countries, while some examined the impact of new technologies on consumer spending (e.g., Dupagne, 1994; Dupagne & Green, 1996; Hedges, 2009; Noh & Grant, 1997).

Data from the *Statistical Abstract* includes information on consumer spending on the media and projections for future years. Estimates for 2009–2011 are presented in Table 9.7; the data represent individual spending for the year in U.S. dollars (rounded).

These data illustrate some interesting trends, taken in context with the previous tables detailing consumer time spent with the media. Here are a few key observations:

- Spending on the media continues to grow each year per person, averaging around a 4% increase per year.

Table 9.7 Projections on U.S. Media Spending (Age 12-Plus, in USD)

CATEGORY	2009	2010	2011
TV (cable/satellite)	375	394	411
Home video	129	132	132
Books	106	108	111
Internet services	59	63	66
Recorded music	44	45	46
Newspapers	47	46	46
Magazines	45	46	46
Box office	44	45	48
Video games	44	47	52
Total spending	929	969	1,010

Note: The table does not include estimates for all media.

Source: Adapted from U.S. Census Bureau (2009).

- Cable and satellite television account for the largest single area of expense, estimated at 40% of consumer media spending. Home video ranks second at around 13%, followed by books at just over 10%.
- Internet services and video games are capturing more spending over time, while newspapers, magazines, and recorded music are trending down.
- Box office spending (movies) is expected to produce small but positive growth.

How does spending relate to household income? For that information we have to use information available online, but not reported in the previous tables. The U.S. Census Bureau estimates that, for 2007 (the most recent available data), the median household income was approximately $50,007, while the size of the average U.S. household was 2.6 (see *Fact sheet*, 2009). In 2007, an estimated $838 was spent per person on the media. Multiplying this number by household size of 2.6 gives a total household spending estimate of $2,179. By dividing total estimated household spending by median household income ($2,179/$50,007), we find that an average of 4.3% was spent on media in the United States, well above the 3% threshold initially identified by McCombs (1972). Of course, this would be expected given the increase in media options, media platforms, and content available in the 21st century.

Caution must be taken when using this broad data. As discussed earlier in this chapter, we know the audience is a collection of many different groups of individuals categorized in various ways by age, gender, income, education, and ethnicity. Thus we know there are numerous differences that are not accounted for in looking at this data from a wide orientation. We know, for example, that variables such as household income influence media usage. As household discretionary income rises, people have more spending power for media products and services. Higher-income households are more likely to subscribe to newspapers than lower-income households. In regard to education, there is typically an inverse relationship with educational level and time spent watching TV; the more educated the individual, the less time spent watching TV. Younger people are much more likely to be heavy users of the Internet in comparison to older adults. And, in terms of ethnicity, new patterns of use are emerging indicating key differences among things like technology use and adoption of social networks (Scarborough Research, 2009).

The data and analysis presented in this chapter provide a broad panorama of individual use and spending on the media, from the perspective of the United States. From this analysis two main observations are clear. First, consumers continue to spend increasing time engaged in media activities. Second, consumers continue to spend more money on the media each year. These two trends clearly illustrate the importance of the individual to the overall media economy.

The question that remains is how much longer will these two areas (time and spending) continue trending upward? Or, stated another way, at what point in time will time and spending on the media begin to flatten or decline? Only with continuing research and analysis can these questions be answered definitively, but one would think that we are probably approaching a tipping point in terms of media usage if for no other reason than the scare resource of time.

THE ISSUE OF "FREE"

The unparalleled growth of the Internet has brought havoc to the media industries, especially for traditional media industries struggling to find ways to compete through alternative digital platforms. As Anderson (2009) discusses, one huge problem traditional media faces is the fact that consumers are used to receiving much of the online content for free, with no investment required. Most consumers scoff at the idea of paying for online content, with astute users knowing that, if the content is not available on one site or platform, they can probably find it elsewhere.

The business model for the recording industry was decimated with the debut of the original Napster peer-to-peer music service that enabled free downloading of music, even if it proved to be an illegal activity. But the end of the original Napster service did not stop illegal downloading. The International Federation of the Phonographic Industry (IFPI) estimates that tens of billions of music files are downloaded illegally each year (IFPI, 2008). The television industry at first resisted offering content online, but eventually gave in and allowed free access to network programs through services like Hulu.com and TV.com. Newspapers moved content quickly to the web, as did many magazines, in hopes of luring readers to their content on the Internet. But, by the fall of 2009, many of these same companies were saying that they were going to have to start charging for content, and that "free" was not a business model that could continue to work.

Anderson (2009) argues that companies will have to offer "freemium" content, meaning some content would be available for free, but premium content would have to be paid for on a per-use or subscription basis. This is not necessarily a new idea, and one that has been tried previously across the media industries by both print and electronic media. But there has been little success. The only model that has proven to be profitable is the online version of the *Wall Street Journal*, with the online content available only through a subscription. The wsj.com site, discussed in Chapter 5, is able to charge for the content because individuals in the financial sector need the information available on a 24/7 basis.

The "freemium" plan may prove ultimately to generate some revenues as a business model for some types of content, but it will be very difficult to encourage consumers to pay for content they are used to finding for free. The plethora of sites offering free content continues to grow each year, and many consumers will simply look to alternatives if their first choice is not available. Recall that the cross-elasticity of media content enables consumers to locate close if not perfect substitutes. Consumer budgets will also have a say in how much individuals will spend on media content; for those used to the free model, there will have to be some compelling needs being met in order for consumers to start paying for content.

SUMMARY

The consumer is a critical component of the media economy, and this chapter has attempted to look at the consumer from a variety of different perspectives in order to understand the social aspects of consumers. Historically, the media industries treated the consumer as a mass entity, but that approach is impossible in the 21st century owing to the fragmentation of the audience brought about by an ever-expanding universe of choice options for media content and products.

Consumers have cultural backgrounds that are unique, depending on the system of norms, beliefs, values, and customs to which they have been exposed. There are differences among consumers in terms of gender, life cycles, and ethnicity, which all contribute to how consumers utilize the media.

Consumers ultimately make decisions on how to allocate their time and spending on the media. The chapter reviewed data on allocation of time and money and found two distinct characteristics: that over the years time spent using media has grown, and that spending on the media has increased each year for individuals. The question that remains is how long will these two patterns continue? Media usage represents the single largest category of activity, and we know that a great deal of media usage is conducted in a multitasking environment.

With many media industries suffering from a loss of audience and the decline of advertising dollars, companies are being forced to rethink how much of their content they can offer for free. As media companies begin charging for their online content, it is uncertain how many consumers will be motivated to pay—especially for content they have been used to obtaining for free. How consumers respond to the option of what Anderson (2009) calls "freemium" content will be a trend to watch and analyze.

If history tells us anything about audiences, it is that they are constantly evolving, not just in terms of age, gender, life cycle, and ethnicity, but also in terms of habits, tastes, and preferences. The media industries find themselves in a very challenging position, as technology enables boundless access and activity, and media companies search for a business model that can sustain their activities. The key difference is that consumers are now in total control of what they access, when they access, and how much they want to spend on media content products and services.

DISCUSSION QUESTIONS

1. Consumers play a pivotal role in the media economy. How does the idea of "consumer media" differ from "mass media"?
2. The section on cultural implications discusses the impact of gender, life cycle, and ethnicity on media behaviors and consumption. Do you agree with some of the findings presented in this part of the chapter? Why or why not?
3. What do we mean by the term "consumer allocation"? How does the concept of allocation impact the media economy?
4. This chapter details two growing trends—spending and time spent with the media continue to grow annually. Do you think these trends will continue? Why or why not?
5. The chapter discusses the problems associated with giving away free content to consumers via the Internet. Some media industries may have to charge for content in order to survive. Do you think consumers will eventually pay for most of the content they access? Would you pay for content? If so, in what areas?

CHAPTER 10

Finance, Valuation, and Investment in the Media Economy

In this chapter you will learn:

- basic aspects of finance and financial management;
- key financial concepts and statements used by business and industry;
- the process of budgeting, and the differences between budgets and capital budgets;
- valuation and models of valuation used in the media economy;
- different categories of investments and their application to the media economy.

This chapter discusses the role of finance, valuation, and investment in the media economy. Any business activity operating with a profit incentive must be concerned about these topics. "Finance" is a broad-based term used to represent the management of money and capital, and how owners and managers monitor the overall financial condition of the business enterprise. If the enterprise is a corporation, this is usually referred to as corporate finance. Valuation is concerned primarily by understanding how much a business is worth, or its overall value in the marketplace. Valuation can look at the entire business entity or focus on one particular segment. Valuation has many uses, ranging from the fair market value of a company to potential mergers and acquisitions to tax liability. Investment represents a set of decisions that companies make with the intent of seeing their business enterprise grow and appreciate. Investment is concerned with ensuring the long-term future of the enterprise, and can encompass many activities from retaining earnings to acquiring new assets. Given this brief introduction to the chapter, we begin our examination of these topics with a look at the role of finance as part of the overall financial management of a business enterprise.

FINANCE AND FINANCIAL MANAGEMENT

In its simplest form, finance refers to the funds that flow in and out of a business entity. Businesses must be aware of all of the financial aspects of their enterprises; most businesses that fail do so as the result of poorly managed finance. Financial management refers to the systematic process of budgeting, monitoring, and controlling the flow of funds in an organization (Albarran, 2009). Financial management is a function at all levels of an organization, with goals and objectives established by the board of directors and its management team.

Financial goals and objectives are usually tied to specific targets, such as a particular quarter or an annual basis. Financial goals and objectives obviously must take into account a number of external factors that can impact any business—the state of the economy, changes in regulatory policy, taxes, technology, and so. The success of a management team is based on the ability of the enterprise to meet or exceed its financial objectives and goals.

In the media economy, meeting financial goals was no problem for many decades. Media industries were thought of as cash machines, but over time increased competition, a host of technological change (as discussed in Chapters 5–6), and the flow of money away from traditional media to online or digital media meant declining revenues. The economic crisis that began in 2007 and continued into 2009 brought an even harsher reality to bear, as media companies faced millions of dollars in lost advertising due to the economy (especially from automotive, retail, and financial services). Media companies recognized the reality of a "new normal" for conducting business, coupled with rising unemployment and tightening credit markets.

Hence, media companies are leaner than they were at the start of the 21st century, meaning fewer employees and, in most cases, smaller revenues. Business is tougher, whether it is selling advertising or obtaining credit. Competition is intense, and every segment of the media industry is concerned with budgets, making their financial goals, and surviving. Thus there has probably never been a greater emphasis on the importance of finance in the media economy as we are experiencing towards the end of the first decade of the 21st century.

BASIC FINANCIAL CONCEPTS

Finance is built on a series of concepts that are used across business activity. This section details some of the concepts used in finance and in financial management, using the media economy as the basis for discussion. Please recognize this is not a complete discussion of finance, but rather a broad introduction. For more detail on business finance, consult additional reference sources and catalogs of existing books at libraries and bookstores.

Assets

Assets represent things that have value and can ultimately be converted into cash. This can range from very "liquid" assets that are easily converted into cash, such as checking and money market accounts, or certificates of deposit and bonds, stock or mutual funds, to more "permanent" assets like buildings, equipment, vehicles, and land. These permanent assets also have value, but may take longer to convert to cash than liquid assets.

Assets can also be intangible, as is the case in the media industries. For example, licenses or franchise and program contracts are considered intangible assets because they hold value, but for specific periods of time. Intellectual property is also an intangible asset. When a movie studio signs a star director to make at least ten feature films over the next five years, the studio is counting on the director's individual creative genius (their acquired intellectual property) to help sell more cinema tickets, DVDs, and rentals. The same is true for actors, recording artists, and authors. Piracy is a huge threat to intellectual property because it is impossible to measure how much potential revenue (assets) is lost due to pirated material.

Generally speaking, companies and their management teams are charged with growing assets, and adding value to the assets over time. Assets are an important part of understanding finance.

Liabilities

Liabilities refer to debt, or money that is owed. Debt is inherent in any business, and businesses operating in the media economy are no exception. Companies can use debt to acquire new assets and expand operations, and for other efforts designed to increase market share. Debt can be used strategically by taking advantage of tax benefits from borrowing. Debt can also be abused, by businesses borrowing too much money, thus creating too much leverage and putting the future of their enterprises in jeopardy. We saw this happen with the financial services industry in 2008, as a number of firms (e.g., Lehman Brothers, Merrill Lynch, Wachovia) either went out of business or were acquired by competitors. Several radio companies (e.g., Clear Channel, Citadel, and

Cumulus) are also suffering from trying to service huge debt loads at a time when advertising has contracted.

There are two types of debt, at least from an accounting standpoint. Short-term liabilities represent obligations that must be repaid in less than one year, while long-term liabilities refer to debt that must be repaid over a longer period of time (e.g., 5, 10, 20, or even 30 years). In acquiring debt, companies should have enough assets to cover all of their debt obligations before borrowing money. When companies take on more debt than they have assets, they are considered to be "overly leveraged," meaning they own more money than can be repaid from their asset base. In acquiring debt, companies strive to obtain the lowest interest rates available, as debt requires repayment of the principal (the amount actually borrowed) plus the interest assigned to the loan.

Credit

Credit involves the lending of capital (money) with the expectation that it will be paid back on a set schedule with interest added to the principal. Media companies extend credit to other vendors and customers as well as use their own credit to borrow money from other lenders.

Internally, media companies engaged in the sale of advertising typically run the advertising as purchased and then issue an invoice for payment. Payment is expected within a 30-day period. In this sense, media companies are extending credit to their clients, giving them time to pay for their advertising after it has run as scheduled. Interest is not charged as long as the invoice is paid on time. These accounts receivable, as they are called in accounting, become part of the asset base, because this category represents money owed to the media company. In the media economy, accounts receivable run on a continuous basis as advertising is contracted across traditional and new media platforms.

Media companies must carefully manage their accounts receivable and, as needed, engage in collections to collect payments that are past due. Accounts that are not paid in a timely manner impact the financial stability of a company. If internal efforts to make collections are not successful, the company may have to turn over the process to an outside collection agency—but this is costly and time-consuming. All of these steps are necessary to try to avoid bad debts—meaning accounts that are never paid.

Externally, media companies utilize credit from lenders to acquire assets. To secure the best terms (interest rates and payback schedule), companies should have established a strong record of credit activity, paying back lenders on schedule, avoiding missed or late payments, and have strong collateral to secure lending. Collateral in this sense represents assets held by the company—land, buildings, equipment, accounts receivable, cash, and other investments, to name a few.

In the business world, there are many possible lenders, although credit tightened considerably after the financial crisis of 2008. Here are a few of the more common sources of credit utilized across the media economy:

- *Commercial lenders.* These are banks and other financial institutions that offer credit and financing to their customers. Commercial lenders are also known as senior lenders, as they represent the most traditional form of lending. These can be short- or long-term obligations, and can come in many forms, ranging from secured loans (tied to collateral) to unsecured loans (no collateral required). Typically, commercial lenders offer the best interest rates, but rates are always subject to market conditions, credit history, and risk.
- *Insurance companies.* Insurance companies represent another source of credit to borrowers. This type of lending is also known as *mezzanine* financing. Debt may be issued in the form of bonds or other financial instruments. This area of credit is more expensive to acquire, meaning that interest rates will be higher than those offered by commercial lenders.
- *Venture capital.* Venture capital is also called equity lending, and is usually reserved for start-ups and other entrepreneurial activity. Venture capital represents the most expensive form of credit; lenders may not just expect to receive their principal repaid with high interest but also require a "stake" in the new company, also known as an equity position—hence the label "equity lending."

Equity

Equity refers to many different things in finance, but here we focus on the term as it is used in financial accounting. Equity simply refers to the ownership of the firm or business. Refer back to our discussion of assets and liabilities. If we use the assets to pay off all the total liabilities and there is money left over, this is referred to as equity or owner's equity (with the owner being the business enterprise or firm and any stockholders or shareholders).

Any company's finances can be thought of as sums of assets, liabilities, and owner's equity. These three interrelated concepts form the components of the most basic financial statement—the balance sheet. Financial statements are discussed next.

FINANCIAL STATEMENTS

Financial statements are used by businesses to monitor financial performance and to comply with established accounting principles. Financial statements are prepared by accountants, and cover activity for a specific time period such as a year, a quarter, a month, or a week. Financial statements are used by many constituents both internally and externally in a business enterprise. Internally, management and department heads use financial statements to track growth, profitability, and performance. Externally, the statements are used by analysts and investors to independently evaluate a company's financial condition.

There are many types of financial statements used in business. You can look at financial statements for a public company online using the company's website (usually found under a link for investor relations), using an electronic database such as LexisNexis, or in a corporation annual report, also found in electronic form and hard copy form at many libraries. Financial statements vary in terms of how they are presented, so not all of them will look exactly the same, but they will contain similar elements. Here are four commonly used financial statements in business according to what the accounting profession refers to as generally accepted accounting principles or GAAP guidelines:

- *Balance sheet.* The balance sheet consists of three segments, all previously discussed in this chapter: assets, liabilities, and owner's equity. On the balance sheet, the assets equal the combined liabilities and owner's equity, hence the term "balance." The balance sheet summarizes the overall financial condition of a firm at a point in time, and allows for easy comparison at different time intervals.
- *Income statement (P&L).* The income statement is also called the profit and loss (P&L) statement, and some texts refer to it as the operating statement. The income statement consists of two distinct areas, the operating revenues and the operating expenses. If revenues exceed expenses (always the preferred situation) then the business has a profit. However, if expenses are greater than revenues, then a loss occurs. The P&L statement identifies where changes in the financial condition of a firm take place over a distinct time period.

- *Statement of cash flows.* The statement of cash flows is used to track the flow of money in a business. This statement lists the sources and actual uses of cash "flows" in a business enterprise, starting with the beginning balance and concluding with the ending balance for a set time period. Virtually all of management is concerned with cash flow, constantly looking for ways to increase cash flow. Cash flow, typically represented as earnings before interest, taxes, depreciation, and amortization (EBITDA), is also a critical variable in determining the value of a media enterprise. Valuation will be discussed later in this chapter.
- *Statement of retained earnings.* The statement of retained earnings is another commonly used financial statement. Of the four statements mentioned in this section, it is often the smallest, as the statement focuses only on the retained earnings or equity position of the company. It summarizes the profit or loss of the enterprise, and reports any dividends paid to shareholders, any profits "retained" by the company, and any other items charged or credited to the business.

Financial statements are validated by an external accounting firm as a step to ensure proper and accurate reporting. In 2002 in the United States, several companies were found to have illegally tampered with their financial statements by reporting inaccurate information and misleading the public (e.g., Enron, Tyco, and WorldCom). In light of this, the U.S. Congress passed the Sarbanes–Oxley Act, which requires each chief executive officer (CEO) personally to attest to the truthfulness and validity of their company's financial statements, or face punishment, including the possibility of imprisonment. "SarBox," as the Act is sometimes called, required a massive overhaul of accounting practices, and forced companies to allocate a great deal more resources to ensuring proper compliance with the new laws. But the law was necessary to calm the fears and anxiety over financial reporting and create greater accountability among publicly held corporations.

BUDGETING AND CAPITAL BUDGETING

Budgeting is a managerial function where companies try to anticipate what their revenues and expenses will be over a period of time—typically the company's next fiscal year. Budgeting involves projections of the future, with the understanding that it is often impossible to predict the future. The budgeting process involves collecting proposed budgets from various units and then compiling them into a master budget, usually with revisions required (Albarran, 2009). Once the budget is set, financial statements are used to ensure that the company is staying on track in meeting its financial goals and objectives, allowing for adjustments to be made as necessary.

There are typically two types of budgets in organizations: the "regular" budget and the capital budget. The differences are simple to understand. The regular budget accounts for the anticipated income and expenses on a day-to-day basis over a period of one year or less. The capital budget is used for the acquisition of expensive equipment, technology, or other larger expenses, which often covers multiple budgetary years or cycles. Capital budgeting is in itself a process that requires analysis of these large purchasing decisions, because most companies cannot make all the capital budgeting acquisitions they want in a single year. Capital budgeting utilizes return on investment tools to identify which potential acquisitions will deliver the most value to the organization. Capital budgeting is sometimes abbreviated or discussed as "cap-ex" expenditures, but it refers to the same type of process.

Budgeting also allows companies to engage in long-term forecasting (estimating long-term revenues) and break-even analysis (identifying how many units of advertising or other income categories must be obtained to cover all necessary expenses). Budgeting requires flexibility as well, so most companies build in some type of contingency budget to allow for unanticipated expenses. This is especially important in the media economy, as the cost of producing news, for example, can jump exponentially depending on domestic or global events.

Depreciation and Amortization

Depreciation and amortization are two terms that have to do with recovering the costs of long-term assets (assets that last longer than one year) over time, such as those discussed under capital budgeting . In the United States, the tax code limits the amount of deductions with certain categories of business investment in equipment and technology in a single year. Many assets such as land, buildings, and vehicles must be depreciated over time.

But what is the difference between depreciation and amortization? Physical or tangible assets are depreciated over time. Intangible assets, such as programming contracts, licenses, franchises, and goodwill, must be amortized over time. But both terms essentially mean the same thing. Depreciation and amortization are deducted from the net income of a business. There are various methods of depreciation and amortization depending on the asset class; as tax rules change over time, businesses must keep aware of changes to their respective tax system that could impact these important deductions to business activity.

Depreciation and amortization are important to businesses because they allow firms to recapture the cost of acquiring assets over time, and also help to lower the amount of tax due for a business enterprise. In this sense, depreciation and amortization are considered "non-cash" adjustments to financial statements, as they contribute to the free cash flow generated in a financial reporting time period.

VALUATION

Valuation is critical in any business or industry, and it takes on unique meanings when applied to the media economy. Valuation is primarily used to evaluate a simple question: How much is the company or firm worth in the market? Valuation is built on both systematic analysis and the principles of supply and demand. Systematic analysis refers to the models used by analysts, brokers, investment bankers, hedge funds, and other interested parties to determine the value of a media enterprise.

Supply and demand also impact valuation. When supply is low and demand is high, the valuation will typically increase. Conversely, if supply is high and demand is low, valuation will usually decrease. There is also the fact that, even though the market estimates the value at a certain level, it does not mean there will be a buyer at that particular price. Let's use a simple real estate example, saying your home is appraised for a fair market value of $250,000. That appraisal—or valuation—is based on current market conditions and factors and reflects the best estimate as to what the house would sell for if placed on the local market. However, you may get offers for less than $250,000 (if supply is high and demand is low) or offers for more than $250,000 (if supply is low and demand is high). Ultimately, the actual selling price will be the result of a negotiation between buyer and seller to determine the final price.

In determining the valuation of media assets, the process is much more complicated than a single real estate transaction but in theory represents a similar idea. In valuing a media property, there are basic assumptions that both the buyer and the seller are motivated to act, that both parties are educated and knowledgeable about the transaction, and that there is adequate time to review all documents and financial statements (Albarran & Patrick, 2005). Where necessary—such as the case of broadcast station transactions—approval for transfer of control from governmental agencies (such as the FCC) is also required. Media valuation differs in terms of the actual models used in the valuation process. These models are discussed in the next section.

MODELS OF VALUATION USED IN THE MEDIA ECONOMY

There are several models used by buyers, sellers, brokers, and analysts in valuing media properties. There are distinctions between broadcast station sales (television and radio) and sales of cable systems and newspapers, which are routinely based on the number of subscribers. Regardless, all models are driven by quantitative metrics, ranging from models to sophisticated models.

Further, most media valuations are based on some multiple of value. A multiple refers to estimated future value of a transaction, and is affected by supply and demand. Multiples are always tied to revenues and cash flow; as demand increases, multiples rise. When demand decreases, the multiple will decline. Multiples are also impacted by other market forces such as interest rates. As rates rise, multiples tend to decline, since the cost of borrowing increases. In broadcast transactions, some multiple is always used in assessing valuation. Broadcast models of valuation are discussed next.

Multiple of Cash Flow

This valuation method is the easiest to understand because it can be calculated with just two variables: the cash flow or EBITDA (usually for the past 12-month time period and found on the income statement) multiplied by the appropriate multiple. For example, if the cash flow for a single radio station in a medium-size market is $3 million, and the multiple is estimated at 7, the station's fair market value would be approximately $21 million. That doesn't mean the station will sell for that amount, but it is considered the market value.

While the EBITDA is easy to locate, the multiple is not something that can be looked up on a financial statement, as a multiple is based on market conditions. As supply tightens and demand rises, the multiples will rise. But, as supply increases and demand softens, multiples will drop. In order to determine the multiple for a specific type of transaction (broadcast, etc.), you have to look at market conditions, current sales (those within the past 6–12 months), and other economic factors. Brokers, financial analysts, and some academic studies also track the status of transaction multiples (see Albarran & Patrick, 2005). Researching previous transactions can also distill trends and average multiples for various classes of transactions.

Multiple of Revenue

The multiple of revenue is a valuation model used where the entity either is a start-up operation or has negative cash flow or insufficient cash flow to make the use of EBITDA possible. Using this model, you take the gross revenues (with no deductions for expenses or other variables like depreciation, interest, taxes, etc.) and apply a conservative multiple, usually no larger than 4. This model is used infrequently, but if the situation involves valuing a distressed or unprofitable enterprise it does offer some utility.

Discounted Cash Flow Model

The discounted cash flow (DCF) model is widely used in assessing the value of a business, including those operating in the media economy. The DCF model is a quantitatively driven model that assesses *future* revenues, expenses, and inflation factors and, using principles from the time value of money, then "discounts" the cash flows back to a present value considering the impact of income taxes and capital expenditures.

DCF models make two critical assumptions—that revenues will rise each year and thus cash flow will also increase. As we have seen in the 21st century with the great volatility in the financial markets and across the media industries, revenues may actually decline over time. Going forward, there is the expectation that traditional media will continue to experience a slow, secular trend of lost advertising and lost circulation (thought of as either viewers or readers depending on the medium).

Albarran and Patrick (2005) provide a detailed examination of the DCF model in their study. The DCF model is the most sophisticated of the three models discussed here, and is widely used across many industries, but it is much more complicated to calculate because of the many variables that must be analyzed.

Albarran and Patrick (2005) also point out that most brokers, especially in the case of broadcast transactions, use all three models but weight them differently to determine the fair market value. Traditionally, according to the authors, the multiples of cash flow and DCF models are each weighted 40%, with the multiple of revenues model accounting for the remaining 20%. Vogel (2007) is another good reference source that details valuation methods across what the author terms "the entertainment" industries. The author points out that most valuation models derive from the use of cash flow and market multiples, but details other variables unique to the industries examined.

INVESTMENT

Investment is another key topic related to finance and valuation, and is important in every industry. Investment, as used in business and finance, simply means anything in which money can be *invested*. An investment decision is made when money is placed in a savings account, or used to buy a stock, bond, or mutual fund. The investment is made with the goal (and hope) of seeing the original investment appreciate over time, and there are numerous investment decisions made in the course of doing business. In this section of the chapter we take a look at some of the key categories of investment decision-making made by firms operating in the media economy.

Public or Private Ownership

The most basic decision regarding investment is whether or not the firm will be a publicly held or private ownership. If the company is a public company, it means its "shares" or "stock" can be acquired by investors in the open market on whatever exchange the firm is listed. Publicly held companies are subject to numerous rules and regulations, and are governed differently from country to country. Publicly held companies are usually known as corporations because the company has legally established formal articles of incorporation.

In the United States, companies incorporate in one of the 50 states. Many companies have chosen to incorporate in Delaware, because the state has no corporate tax and offers other incentives. Investors, consisting of both institutional and individual investors, elect the board of directors and vote on various amendments and changes to the charter proposed by both the company and investors. Institutional investors consist of entities like insurance firms, retirement funds, and other corporations, to name a few. Public companies must hold annual meetings with their stockholders, and file appropriate financial documents and reports as required.

Privately held companies differ in that they do not offer any shares in the public market, as all ownership is controlled by private investors. Privately held companies, unlike publicly held companies, are not required to file financial statements and quarterly reports, nor are they required to hold annual meetings. Private companies do establish themselves as corporations, because they are still subject to taxes and other laws pertaining to business entities.

Historically, most companies operating in the media economy

became public companies, although in the 21st century several buyouts from private investors turned large previously held public companies (e.g., Univision, Clear Channel Communications) into private entities, especially in the United States. Why did this happen? Several reasons have been offered for this trend.

First, "Wall Street" had become disenchanted with traditional media, feeling their best years were behind them as consumers migrated to the Internet and other digital platforms. Second, as advertising and ratings or circulation declined, profit margins began to fall, while investors were still demanding higher returns. On Wall Street, a company is only as good as its most recent quarterly return, making it hard for companies to focus on a long-term strategy when new profits are expected every 90 days from the investment community and the stockholders. Facing this pressure and frustration, some companies began to "sell out" and move to private status.

It is too early to tell if this is going to be a continuing trend, or more of an anomaly. In the case of both Univision and Clear Channel, the massive debt obligations held by their new owners have continued to hurt their financial performance since the deals were finalized. Coupled with the financial crisis that hit America in 2008, credit for new acquisitions has tightened, making it harder to put together large deals.

Stock

For publicly held companies, decisions must also be made on the type of stock to issue or offer to the open market. Two types of stock are typical: common stock and preferred stock. Common stock is what most individual investors acquire when they purchase corporate stock through an online account or a broker. Common stock may be offered in different types of classes. For example, Viacom offers class "B" shares of common stock for sale to individual investors on the New York Stock Exchange (NYSE).

Preferred stock is a higher class of stock than common stock, and is often restricted as to who can actually purchase the shares (often institutional investors or internal investors over regular investors). Preferred stock owners have some advantages over common stock owners in that they have priority over common stock owners in two areas: the event of payment of any dividends (discussed below) and the chance to regain their investment first in the event of a liquidation. In the case of a dividend, preferred holders usually receive a higher dividend than holders of common stock.

Other Stock Considerations

In addition to determining the classes of stock to make available to the open market, companies must also decide if they will offer a dividend to be paid to investors on a quarterly basis. Dividends represent a portion of the company's profits, and are also referred to as the dividend yield. Recall that retained earnings represent when a company chooses to reserve some of its profits; dividends thus represent profits that are returned to investors in the form of a quarterly payment.

For example, if a company has a dividend of $1 per share, it will pay that dividend in four quarterly payments of 25 cents per share. Dividends are important to investors because they represent a return on their investment and, along with any appreciation, add to the value of owning stocks. For example, if you buy 100 shares of a hypothetical entity called Media ABC at $10 a share, your investment is $1,000. Media ABC pays a 3% dividend—meaning in this case 30 cents, or four quarterly payments of 7.5 cents per share. Let's say that after a year the stock of Media ABC has risen by 5%, so it is now trading at $10.50 a share. You are still getting your 3% dividend, and the stock has appreciated, so your original investment is worth $1,050. Your rate of return for the year, considering both the dividends received for the year and the appreciation of the shares, is 8%. Of course, you realize this gain only if you sell your shares in Media ABC—and the sale of the stock is subject to capital gains and other taxes—but you can see how dividends and appreciation of stock create long-term value.

But, as many of us experienced in the painful economic recession of 2008, not only did stocks fall in value but hundreds of companies cut or completely eliminated dividends to save cash and improve their balance sheets in the volatile economy. It is expected that many companies, including those in the media economy, will be very slow to reinstate dividends as the economy improves, simply because of the fear of another downturn and the challenges of acquiring future capital (Zuckerman, 2009).

Stock Repurchases

Another consideration for companies is the repurchasing of their own stock or shares. The primary motivation in repurchasing shares of stock is to increase the market value of the shares, and this has been done in periods of both expansion and decline. When a company repurchases its own shares, this effectively reduces the shares held by the public. If profits remain the same as before the repurchase, this would increase the actual earnings per share because the earnings are the same but the number of shares is lower. The strategy of repurchasing shares, especially during depressed economic conditions, can increase the return on investment for the stock. In the U.S. alone, there are several methods of doing a stock repurchase, including repurchasing on the open market. Another impact of the 2008 recession has been fewer repurchasing buybacks, as companies continue to hold cash (Zuckerman, 2009).

Stock Splits

A stock split occurs when a company increases or decreases the number of shares of its stock. In either case, the price is adjusted after the split so that the market capitalization remains the same. In a stock split, the company increases the number of shares outstanding. In a 2–1 stock split the company would award an additional share of stock to each share of stock already held by an investor, so, if an investor had 100 shares before the split, a 2–1 split would give the investor 200 shares. For example, if the pre-split price is $20 a share, the price after the split would be $10 per share. The company has in this case doubled the number of shares outstanding, but it has not affected the overall value of the company. A firm uses a stock split historically either when its price gets too high compared to other competitors in the same market or to attract smaller investors.

A reverse split works the opposite way. In this case the company has probably had a declining stock price, and engages in a reverse split to increase the price per share. If a company issues a 10–1 reverse split, an investor holding 100 shares of stock would own only 10 shares following the split. If the pre-reverse split price was 25 cents a share, the post-split price rises to $2.50 a share. As with the regular split, the market capitalization for the firm remains the same, but the number of outstanding shares is lowered. Reverse splits are usually approved by a firm's board of directors when the company is in severe financial distress.

Research and Development

Related to the topic of investment is the question of how much of the firm's cash resources will be reinvested in research and development. Research and development expenditures, or R&D as it is commonly known, vary across industries. In some fields, such as pharmaceuticals and technology, billions are spent on R&D every year. Companies operating in the media economy must also invest in R&D, depending of course on the areas of engagement. A content-oriented company will invest resources in developing new programming, content for different platforms, and ways to improve existing content. A distribution company will invest more in technology-related R&D in order to improve options for consumers and increase bandwidth and storage capacity. Telecommunication firms are constantly investing in R&D, and their work has enabled innovations in things like fiber optics and smart phones. Generally speaking, companies will typically invest a percentage of their revenues in R&D similar to amounts spent by competitors.

Future Acquisitions

Another form of investment occurs when firms make acquisitions of other firms, via a merger or an acquisition. Just about every major company that exists in the media economy grew by acquisition of other companies. Acquisitions that strengthen the core of a company allow it to engage in economies of scale; economies of scope can also be realized by giving firms a foothold in horizontally related industries. Acquisitions come about by opportunities, and to be ready companies need to carefully manage their investments and raise capital as needed when the situation warrants.

SUMMARY

This chapter examined the role of finance, valuation, and investment found in business and industry, with examples found across the media economy. Finance is a broad-based concept encompassing the tools associated with financial management, tracking the money that flows in and out of a company. A number of key concepts were introduced in discussing finance, including the differences between assets, liabilities, credit, and equity. Basic financial statements were introduced in the form of the balance sheet, the income statement (also known as the P&L statement), the statement of cash flows, and the statement of retained earnings.

Budgeting is a tool used to anticipate revenues and expenditures, and is an annual exercise for all companies. Companies have their annual or regular budget, but also prepare a separate capital budget for the acquisition of long-term assets (those over one year of age). Depreciation and amortization were introduced as two means to cover the cost of tangible and intangible assets acquired as a result of the budgeting process.

Valuation has many meanings in business and economics, and in this chapter valuation was discussed by focusing on how to determine the fair market value of a media enterprise. Supply and demand impact valuation, as do market conditions. The basic models of valuation used in the media industries were presented, including the multiple of cash flow, the multiple of revenues, and the discounted cash flow model. The role of the "multiple" was also introduced and explained in the context of conducting valuation analysis.

Finally, this chapter examined investment from the perspective of decision-making around investment topics. Among the investment decisions discussed were: the differences between public and private ownership; decisions on the different types of stock to offer for sale; the consideration of establishing dividends; stock repurchases and stock splits; research and development; and future acquisitions.

Knowledge of finance, valuation, and investment is critical in understanding the economic aspects of the media economy, but a basic understanding of these topics is also helpful in everyday life to understand our own personal finance. Because of changes in tax laws and other legal regulations, it is critical for companies—and individuals—to maintain continuing education in each of these areas.

DISCUSSION QUESTIONS

1. What is financial management, and how is it used in business and industry?
2. Financial statements play an important role both internally and externally for an organization. Discuss how financial statements are used internally, and how they are used by others external to the enterprise.
3. How does the "regular" budgeting process differ from the capital budgeting process? How are capital budgeting decisions made?
4. Most valuation models used in the media economy are tied to the concept of cash flow. What is cash flow, and why is it so important in assessing valuation of a media property?
5. Investment decisions for business and industry differ from the decisions we make as individuals. What are some of the investment decisions made by a business enterprise? How are these decisions interpreted by the financial community and potential investors?

CHAPTER 11

Labor and the Media Economy

In this chapter you will learn:

- why labor and employment are important components of the media economy;
- the limited research findings that exist on labor and the media economy;
- key employment trends and patterns in the United States;
- trends in media employment in the United States from 1990 to 2009.

A key economic indicator in any country is that of employment. Employment provides a labor force to do the work of companies, and the wages earned provide for an individual's standard of living and generate consumption (spending) and savings. Governments levy taxes on employers and employees through various types of labor taxes; these tax revenues pay for all types of government spending. Job creation and growth are critical in every economy, and are a common goal shared by both government and the private sector. Employment is not something to be taken for granted, as any country that experiences high levels of unemployment will attest.

THE GLOBAL EMPLOYMENT SITUATION

Labor and employment trends are topics that have traditionally been followed by economists, working either in the government or in the private sector. Labor can be categorized in many ways. The International Labour Organization (ILO, www.ilo.org), a non-profit group that collects data on employment for over 200 countries, uses broad categories of agriculture, services, and industry (manufacturing) to differentiate employment.

According to the ILO, the estimated total global employment as of late 2009 was estimated at 2.8 billion people (age 15-plus), while an estimated 200-plus million people were unemployed, indicating a global unemployment rate rising above 6% (ILO, 2008). The years 2008 and 2009 resulted in negative job growth, owing to the global recession.

In December 2007, the United States—and many other industrialized nations—had slipped into what would be a devastating recession. The recession proved to be much deeper and wider than anyone could have predicted. By the end of 2008, stock markets and economies around most of the globe had plunged, reaching their low point in March 2009. The United States experienced its worst economic time since the depression era of 1931, coupled with a mass housing and financial crisis as well as volatility in the price of crude oil.

The situation in the United States caused a major shift in labor, as companies terminated thousands of jobs in an effort to cut costs and stay in business. The U.S. unemployment rate jumped to 7.2% by the end of 2008, topping 10% in 2009. Higher unemployment also became the norm in many other regions of the world, according to the ILO (2008). The strong growth in employment the world experienced between 1997 and 2007 reversed trends in 2008 and 2009, as global unemployment grew.

EMPLOYMENT IN THE MEDIA ECONOMY

This discussion and overview of global employment trends gives us reason to ask a basic question: What is the employment situation in the media economy? This chapter examines employment in the media economy, with an emphasis on the United States, utilizing a select group of media industries. As one of the largest developed countries in the world, the United States is also one of the globe's largest employers in the world, with an estimated 138.8 million people working in the country in non-agriculture and non-military occupations as of November 2009.

The United States is also widely recognized as the long-term global leader in media, evidenced by the voluminous amount of content generated in the form of television and radio programs, motion pictures, newspapers, books and magazines, sound recordings, and websites. The United States has been labeled an "entertainment economy" (Wolf, 1999), as content generated in Hollywood and other cities spans the globe.

However, there has been little examination of media-related

employment in the scholarly literature, either in the United States or globally. What studies do exist have a tendency to focus on topics related to surveys of new graduates seeking industry employment. A few studies look at the topic of employment from the standpoint of analyzing skills needed by employers for specific types of positions. Data-based papers showing employment trends are simply not available. Further, many trade associations for specific media industries lack accurate and timely employment-related data.

This chapter attempts to provide some data on U.S. media employment by analyzing a 17-year period of employment from 1990 through 2009. First, we present the available literature on media employment for review and discussion.

MEDIA EMPLOYMENT RESEARCH

The following is a review of previous research and literature on employment in the media industries. A large portion of the literature focuses on the ability of new college and university graduates to locate employment in an area related to their field.

Becker (1992) found that the unemployment rate among journalism and mass communication graduates in the U.S. went up in 1990, citing possible causes as a recession in the national economy and the influx of a record number of journalism and mass communication graduates into the labor market. The study concluded that more journalism and mass communication students than ever before were looking for work.

Giles (1993) explored trends in the newspaper industry, including the restructuring and rethinking of management, news coverage, advertising, and hiring practices. These changes were warranted by changes in customer needs because customers had more choices than ever before. When old models and expectations of increasing profits through customer sales no longer proved sufficient, the newspaper industry's focus shifted to marketing and research tools to attract advertisers. Newspapers also became faced with new challenges in how they managed their workforce, particularly in areas such as performance standards and technology.

Hilt and Lipschultz (1996) studied career preparation needed for broadcast newsroom hiring. The study surveyed two groups, students who completed a broadcast internship, and hiring managers in the industry. Students were surveyed during the last week of their internships as part of a weekly meeting they attended to discuss internship progress. Between 1993 and 1995, students were queried about their opinion on a variety of items, including factors affecting their likelihood to be hired as well as what they considered the most essential job skills in their industry. Student responses were then compared to an earlier mail survey administered to newsroom employers. Both groups reported writing, listening, oral communication, self-motivation, and dedication as very important skills for working in a broadcast newsroom. Employers considered news judgment of great importance, while students placed emphasis on college degree and major. But employers reported that these were among their least important factors in influencing hiring decisions. The study offers broad implications regarding instructional methods and effectiveness, questioning the value and correct mix of theory, skills training, and liberal arts content in broadcast news degree programs.

Becker, Lauf, and Lowrey (1999) studied the correlation between affirmative action programs and hiring practices in the journalism and mass communication labor market. Intended as an assessment of social policies and their effects as well as a development of social and organizational theory, this study was administered via a mailed questionnaire to bachelor and master degree recipients at a sampling of schools from the Association for Education in Journalism and Mass Communication's (AEJMC) annual *Journalism and Mass Communication Directory*. The study queried graduates about a number of items including job seeking, salary and benefits, and university experiences. It concluded that the journalism and mass communication industry still needs affirmative action programs, finding that informal hiring practices tended indirectly to discourage the hiring of minorities. Race and ethnicity proved to be a negative predictor of hiring success among graduates. But it also cautioned that this particular situation in the journalism and mass communication labor market is a complex issue and warrants further study.

Berryman (2004) explored how the digital world, particularly the Internet, has changed the role of the radio producer in Australia. According to the author, the repackaging of audio for online delivery has become paramount in this changing role. Berryman reports on a degree program at one Australian university that prepares students for these changes.

Farhi (2006) investigates how bad the state of affairs was for newspaper industry employees in 2006. According to Farhi, the issue appears even more problematic when examined in context over the past couple of decades, and 2005 was almost as bad as the record worst period for the industry during the national economic recession in 1991–1993. Recounting how the industry has survived major upheavals before, the author warns that the newspaper industry needs to protect and preserve its legacy of daily reporting while also reinventing itself to adapt to changing times in order to compete with the wide variety of other media outlets.

Speckman (2006) found that the journalism job market was on the rebound and better for new college graduates, with more entry-level jobs available than in the previous five years. However, openings for mid-level journalism jobs were rarer.

EMPLOYMENT IN THE UNITED STATES

In order to understand employment in the specific media sectors operating in the United States, it is first helpful to understand basic employment patterns and trends in the country. The best source that exists on employment in all sectors of the U.S. economy is a government agency, the Bureau of Labor Statistics (BLS). The BLS aggregates data from numerous industry sources, and is the primary source of labor employment statistics in America.

It is helpful to understand how many people are actually employed in the United States, across all sectors of industry and work. Towards the end of 2009, approximately 138 million people were employed in civilian occupations in the United States, as shown in Figure 11.1. The "civilian" group includes all private industry and state and local government workers. Federal government, military, and agricultural workers are excluded. As can be seen in Figure 11.1, civilian employment slowly trended upwards until 2000, followed by a slight decline, and

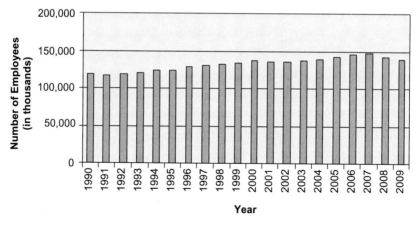

Figure 11.1 Civilian Employment in the United States, 1990–2009

Source: Bureau of Labor Statistics.

Note: 2009 data estimated in all figures based on first ten months of the year.

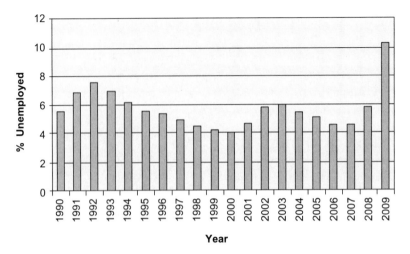

Figure 11.2 Trends in Unemployment in the United States, 1990–2009

Source: Bureau of Labor Statistics.

then peaked at 146 million employed in 2007, only to fall dramatically in 2008 owing to the national recession.

Another widely used metric to look at labor issues is the unemployment rate. The unemployment rate is expressed as a simple percentage, and details how many Americans are out of work, filing claims within the various states they live in for unemployment compensation. Unemployment statistics do not include those people in the population who are retired, who choose not to work, or who are too young to work. This data is detailed in Figure 11.2.

Historically, the unemployment rate in the United States has averaged around 5%, with higher rates reported in years associated with recessions. Since 1990, the unemployment rate in the United States hit a previous peak of 7.4%, in 1992, and reached its trough in 2000 at 3.9%. However, by the end of 2008, the unemployment rate had risen to 7.2%, jumping to 10.2% in October 2009. The unemployment rate is both an economic and a political issue, with the data used in political circles and by labor unions and other employment groups to illustrate their causes and concerns.

EMPLOYMENT IN THE MEDIA SECTORS IN THE UNITED STATES
The BLS aggregates all media-related employment under the broad industrial category of information. The information sector includes: publishing; broadcasting; motion pictures and sound recordings;

telecommunications; data processing, hosting, and related services; and other information services. In 1990, total employment in the information sector was 2.69 million, peaking at 3.71 million in March 2001. By the end of 2008, employment across the sector had fallen to 2.95 million employees. With total employment at 144 million in 2008, this means labor in the media economy represented approximately 2% of the U.S. workforce. Let's take a closer look at the six sub-sectors of the larger information classification used by the BLS.

Publishing Industries

The BLS includes several different industries under the heading of "publishing," such as employment in newspapers, magazines, and book publishing. Internet publishing is *not* included in this sector. Figure 11.3 presents trends in publishing employment in the United States from 1990 to 2009.

As seen in Figure 11.3, employment in the publishing sector peaked in 2000 with just over 1 million employees engaged in some aspect of publishing. Since 2000, there has been considerable contraction in the publishing sector, as employment in 2001 dropped 4.9% from 2000, another 4.3% decline in 2002, and a 3.9% decline in 2003. In the next four years (2004–2007), publishing industry jobs declined another 2.4%. In 2008, the jobs declined another 4.1%, to 856,000 jobs, falling to under 800,000 jobs in 2009.

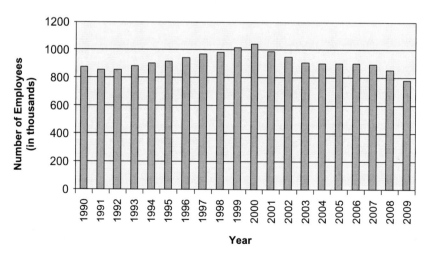

Figure 11.3 Employment in Publishing Industries, 1990–2009

Source: Bureau of Labor Statistics.

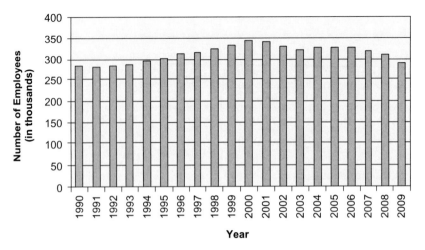

Figure 11.4 Trends in Broadcast Employment, 1990–2009

Source: Bureau of Labor Statistics.

Broadcast Industry

The broadcast industry encompasses traditional television and radio stations, networks, and associated entities, as well as cable television and other subscription-based programming services. Here the BLS data is not as broad and inclusive as for the publishing industry, and offers a clearer picture of employment. Broadcasting is one of the smallest media sectors in the United States in terms of employment. As in the publishing industry, employment peaked during the 2000–2001 years, with over 340,000 people employed in some aspect of the broadcasting industry.

Since 2002, reduction in employment has occurred on an annual basis, much of it related to continuing downsizing and cost cutting as the radio industry tried to grow revenues. By 2009, the number of jobs in the broadcast industry had fallen below 300,000, its lowest level since 1994. The data on broadcast employment is presented in Figure 11.4.

Motion Pictures and Sound Recording Industries

The BLS data combines the motion picture industry with the sound recording industry in monitoring employment statistics; thus it is a challenging area to investigate. The data includes many sub-areas aside from the actual production of motion pictures and sound recordings. For example, in the motion pictures area, the data encompasses film

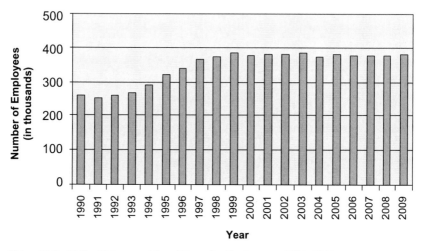

Figure 11.5 Motion Pictures and Sound Recording Employment, 1990–2009

Source: Bureau of Labor Statistics.

production, services related to the film industry, and employment in movie theaters, while the sound recording area involves producers, technicians, and different production techniques. Employment in these sectors peaked at 385,000 in 2003, but has remained relatively flat since that time. Figure 11.5 details employment trends from 1990 to 2009 in this media sector.

Telecommunications Industry

The telecommunications industry is made up of a number of sub-sectors that are critical to understanding employment in the media economy. The BLS data on the telecommunications industry includes such areas as telephony (both fixed and wireless phones), voice over Internet protocol (VOIP), cable and satellite distribution, and Internet access. Figure 11.6 details trends in telecommunications employment since 1990.

Telecommunications represents the largest sector of employment in the media economy, fueled by: the expansion of mobile phones; video distribution by telecommunications companies; growth among cable, satellite, and IPTV; VOIP distribution; and Internet access companies. Peak employment occurred in 2000, with approximately 1.46 million jobs. Since that time, employment has contracted, with over 400,000 jobs lost by 2009, when employment dropped below 1 million jobs. As with other sectors, the job losses are related to a recessionary economy, corporate downsizing of personnel, and consolidation.

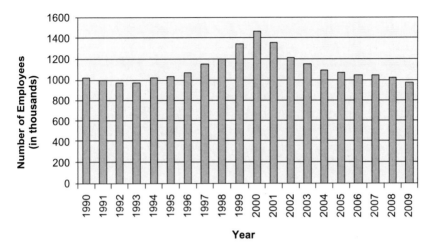

Figure 11.6   Telecommunications Industry Employment, 1990–2009

Source: Bureau of Labor Statistics.

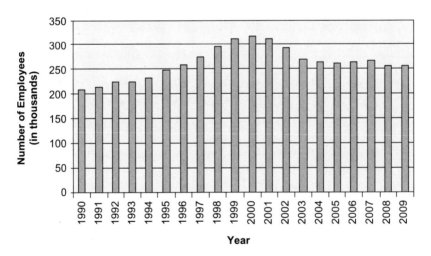

Figure 11.7   Data Processing, Hosting, and Related Services, 1990–2009

Source: Bureau of Labor Statistics.

Data Processing, Hosting, and Related Services

The BLS formerly used a category called "Internet service providers, Web search, and data processing services" to define employment in these sub-sectors, but changed the name of this sector to "data processing, hosting, and related services" in 2007. According to the

BLS, some of the historical data reflects the older definitions. Still, it provides a useful benchmark of employment in what is for the most part jobs related to the Internet in the United States. The data on this sector is found in Figure 11.7.

Employment in these areas grew rapidly from 1990 to 2000, when the number of jobs increased by 50%, from slightly over 200,000 jobs to over 318,000. However, since 2000, we again see a clear contraction of employment, as the number of jobs in this sector had shrunk by nearly 57,000 by November 2009. Part of the drop in employment in this area was due to the overall collapse of the dot-com bubble in 2001, which took a severe toll on the job market from which it never recovered. As in the other sectors, the recession of 2008 and 2009 also contributed to the erosion of more jobs.

Other Information Services

The final sub-category of the information sector on the BLS website reflects employment in a number of key areas to the media economy. This sub-sector includes such things as web search portals, news syndicators, and exclusive (Internet only) publishing and broadcasting, as well as libraries and archives.

As seen in Figure 11.8, this sector consisted of only 60,000 jobs in 1990, but ten years later the number of jobs had grown to over 158,000. Once again, contraction is evident after 2000 following the dot-com

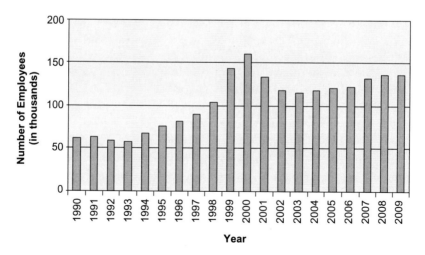

Figure 11.8 Other Information Services, 1990–2009

Source: Bureau of Labor Statistics.

collapse. Jobs declined by over 25,000 in 2001, only to fall by 26,000 more in 2002. However, the employment in this sub-sector had fared better by 2008, with employment again growing to around 135,000 jobs by late 2009.

DISCUSSION AND CONCLUSIONS

This chapter describes employment patterns in the various media sectors operating in the United States of America from 1990 to 2009, using public data compiled by the U.S. government's Bureau of Labor Statistics. In order first to understand employment in America, the chapter presented an examination of data related to civilian employment and also reviewed the level of unemployment reported from 1990 to 2009. The American economy, like many economies, is driven in large part by employment and consumer spending in various sectors. The United States has also transitioned since the country was founded from an agrarian economy to an industrial economy to what is now an information and services economy early in the 21st century.

In the United States, there were approximately 139 million people employed across the country as of late 2009. In regard to the six sub-areas of the information sector, approximately 2.9 million people were employed in the U.S. late in 2009. Stated another way, the media economy employs approximately 2% of the people in the country. As we saw in Chapter 1, the U.S. media industries accounted for approximately 2.66% of the nation's GDP as of 2008. The fact that the media employment base is 2% of the population—yet contributes more than that according to GDP—shows the media industries to be operating very efficiently in the U.S. economy. One caveat—the analysis of media revenues to GDP in Chapter 1 *did not include* the telecommunications sector. According to data from the World Bank for 2007 (latest available data), the U.S. telecommunications sector accounted for 3.1% of total U.S. GDP (World Bank, 2009). Therefore, we can estimate that total GDP in the media economy, with the inclusion of the telecommunications sector, probably accounts for somewhere around 5.6–5.7% of the nation's total GDP. This data makes the contribution of the media economy to the nation's GDP even greater and more meaningful, provided we include the contribution of the telecommunications sector.

Within the various areas that make up the media industries identified in this chapter, it is clear that employment has contracted or flattened across all sectors, including the Internet. In the media industries, several factors have contributed to the overall decline of employment, and these are discussed below.

Consolidation has been one key factor. During the expansion of the U.S. economy in the 1990s, the large number of mergers and acquisitions often resulted in a reduction of employees to eliminate duplication of job functions. As employees are the most expensive part of any organization, efforts to trim payrolls and control costs are critical among any business operations, including the media. Reducing payroll eliminates salaries, benefits, and employer taxes.

Technology has also led to a decline in jobs, especially in areas like media-related production. For example, today a television news reporter often reports a story from a field location alone; the reporter shoots and packages the story, does any necessary editing, and uploads the story via the Internet. Just a few years ago, it would take a reporter, a photographer, a lighting technician, and even a writer and editor to do the same story. Multiple processes can be managed by fewer employees in a digital environment, leading to leaner departments and people skilled in multitasking.

Globalization also shares some of the blame. The U.S. is among the nations with the highest cost of employment, especially given the presence of many guilds and craft unions which require higher pay scales. In the motion picture sector, "runaway productions" is a term used to identify movies shot outside of the U.S. for this very reason. Where feasible, other job functions can be outsourced to other countries to save money.

Finally, economic conditions clearly impact employment in the media economy. When there is broad economic contraction across the economy, many jobs are lost. The BLS estimates total employment dropped from 144 million in 2008 to 139 million in 2009, a loss of 5 million jobs. Advertising Age reported that the U.S. media had cut more than 196,000 jobs since 2000, an estimated 18.6%, with the largest losses taking place in the newspaper industry, where over 109,700 jobs were lost (Advertising Age, 2008).

What do these changes mean for the future of the media industries? One obvious change is that the media industries are doing more with less, in terms both of revenues and of personnel. There are fewer jobs available, and the decline is likely to continue. By the end of 2008, several media companies had moved into Chapter 11 bankruptcy—the Tribune Company in publishing and Pappas Telecasting in broadcast TV, to offer just a couple of examples. Over the next few years, it is very probable that several radio and newspaper companies will simply cease to exist. In short, we can expect more contraction in employment across the media industries.

These changes will also present challenges for colleges and universities that are training graduates for employment in some aspect of the media. As employment continues to contract in traditional industries, a new emphasis on generating and distributing content across multiple platforms is now the norm. In all likelihood, there will be fewer employment opportunities in traditional media in the years ahead, but far greater opportunities for people who can work in different media modalities across different media platforms. This will mean, among other things, changing and refining university curriculums and degree requirements to meet the changing employment nature of the media industries and ancillary fields.

History also tells us that the media industries adapt to change, although at times the pace seems rather slow. Newspapers and radio have had to redefine themselves many times, especially with the debut of television in the 1940s and 1950s; today these same industries—along with television—are redefining themselves in the information age dominated by the Internet. By understanding how this transformation takes place, we will have a clearer picture of how this will affect and impact future employment in the media sectors operating in the United States, and globally as well.

More ongoing research on media-related employment is needed to follow trends and patterns in the media economy. Too little attention has been paid to employment trends in the media, and hopefully some of the data in this chapter will provide some initial trends and benchmarking data for other scholars to build upon in the future.

DISCUSSION QUESTIONS

1. How was employment in the U.S. and globally impacted by the recession of 2008?
2. Why have there been so few studies examining labor and employment in the media economy? What are the reasons for the lack of research?
3. Media employment in the United States shows a flat or downward trajectory since 2001 in most sectors. What has been the cause of this flattening or retraction in employment? What do you see as the challenges this data presents for those seeking to enter the field?
4. The findings of this chapter suggest that the U.S. media industries contribute positively to the country's GDP. How was this determined? Discuss.
5. Based on the information in this chapter, what advice would

you offer potential employees who want to enter the media industries about employment opportunities? Do you think certain sectors offer more potential than others? Which ones and why?

CHAPTER 12

Assessing the Future of the Media Economy

In this chapter you will learn:

- what we know about the media economy;
- why the media economy is in transformation;
- what is "the new normal" and how it applies to the media economy;
- suggestions for new research on the media economy.

This chapter provides a summary and synthesis of this volume in order to clarify the state of knowledge on the media economy, and also to offer some propositions to guide future research and study. One must recognize that the media economy is a continually evolving phenomenon, constantly adapting and changing in response to the various forces outlined in this text. Thus we can never "capture" at any specific point in time what the media economy is, but we can identify trends and patterns to help us understand how the media economy is evolving and changing.

THE STATE OF KNOWLEDGE ON THE MEDIA ECONOMY

The study of the economic aspects of the media industries began in earnest in the 1950s, so a considerable body of knowledge exists to aid us in looking back at this field of study and drawing conclusions based on this earlier work. Taking a very broad and sweeping approach to describing the state of knowledge in the media economy over the past 60 years, here are the key points of what is known:

- While the study of the media economy grew out of macroeconomic, microeconomic, and critical perspectives,

most of the scholarship published within the three areas
does not consider the impact of the other two areas in their
analysis. Each area has tended to operate in isolation,
with an even greater divide separating the critical
perspective.

- As for the macroeconomics and microeconomics dimensions,
  the bulk of inquiry has been at the microeconomic level. One
  obvious reason for this is the lack of good data at the national
  level, although this situation has improved thanks to more
  researchers working globally and the sharing of knowledge via
  the Internet.

- Most of the theories used to analyze the media economy are
  drawn from other fields of study, with economics providing
  the primary contribution. There has been some theory
  development that has taken place, but more effort must be done
  to establish and develop theories to capture the essence of the
  holistic media economy that operates across multiple levels of
  society.

- The methodological tools used to study the media economy have
  become more sophisticated over time, but the challenge of the
  digital age brings the opportunity for still greater development.
  There are specific areas of the media economy (e.g., global,
  national) that need better tools of analysis along with more
  reliable data sources.

- The literature is well represented in terms of studies focused on
  traditional media like publishing and broadcasting, and there is
  a growing body of research on digital and new media. Moving
  forward, most of the scholarly work will likely focus on new
  media as well as new media's continuing impact on traditional
  media.

- Likewise, the literature is well represented in terms of studies
  conducted in North America, Western Europe, Australia, and
  key Asian nations like Japan and South Korea. An emerging
  body of new international research is building from China, Latin
  America, and some Eastern European nations. Asia (especially
  India), Africa, and the Middle East are areas for potential
  development and expansion in the 21st century.

- Research on the media economy has become more critical to
  policymakers over the years, as governments struggle with the
  questions of how to define markets, assess competition, and
  determine future regulation.

THE MEDIA ECONOMY IN TRANSFORMATION

Clearly the media economy is in a state of transformation. Transformation is defined as an act or a process that transforms something, resulting in a change in form or appearance (*Transformation*, n.d.). As part of this transformation process, traditional media continues its migration and adaptation to new digital platforms, business models are refined and adapted, and new media companies emerge.

This text has shown how the converging forces of economics, technology, globalization, regulation, and social aspects are all influencing the transformation process of the media economy. This is evident when regulators attempt to deal with the ever more challenging task of how to define markets. Our understanding of markets must expand and be more sensitive to technological change and innovation. Markets are everywhere in the media economy, and there are numerous suppliers offering their goods and services at all levels of activity.

Consumers are also part of this transformation process. Consumers have learned to adapt and adopt new technological innovations involving reception technologies for use at home and work and on the go. Consumers play a pivotal role in the transformation of the media economy, not just in terms of their tastes and preferences, but also in their allocation of time (attention) and expenditures on media-related products and services.

Given the continuing advancements in technology, as well as the entrepreneurial expertise surrounding the media and communications industries, this transformation process may never be complete. The media economy appears to be in an ever-evolving state of transformation and change at all levels, impacting not only those companies that develop content goods and services but also those that consume the goods and services, namely consumers and advertisers.

THE NEW NORMAL AND GOING FORWARD

One result of the global economic recession that began in the fall of 2007 and continued through 2008 and much of 2009 was the realization that moving forward things would never be the same in terms of the economy and the financial world. A phrase appeared to describe this situation, "the new normal." Who exactly was the first to either write or speak the words "the new normal" cannot be clearly identified by this author; run your favorite search engine and you will find thousands of references to this phrase, but nothing definitive as to who said it first. But it is not who said it first that is as important to our purposes as to understanding what the new normal means for the media economy.

The new normal for the media economy means change and evolution across levels and many areas of doing business. Here are a few areas where the new normal exists in the media economy:

- Traditional media, with the exception of television, has likely peaked in terms of advertising revenues. This means that going forward the new normal for most areas of media advertising will be a slow, secular decline. New media, primarily the Internet and select digital platforms that utilize subscription or pay-per-use models, will likely continue to grow advertising.
- The contraction of advertising poses huge problems for newspapers, radio, magazines, and local television. These media must identify new revenue streams while continuing to keep tight control on costs. For these areas, the new normal means less revenue, and could lead to a greater loss in perceived quality and value among consumers.
- Social media will emerge as one of the main drivers to other media. All companies must have a strong presence among social media, and use social media to drive awareness and interest in media products and services. Social media will also become a growing source of advertising revenue for those companies engaged in the industry (e.g., Facebook, Twitter, LinkedIn, MySpace, etc.).
- In addition to social media, mobile media will continue to grow, fueled by the sale and expansion of smart phones. Video will also be a key driver, especially online video accessed via a television receiver or through one of the many platforms available for distribution and consumption.
- New business models need development that can ultimately prove to be sustainable as the competitive environment continues to evolve. The new business models will build on incremental revenues (Anderson, 2006), as well as subscription-based models and pay-per-use models.
- As we have seen happen with a number of newspapers, many smaller media operations will be forced out of business. In some respects, this will help eliminate part of the excess, and the survivors will benefit from the demise of some competitors.
- In the old normal the trend was toward expansion and consolidation among media companies. In the new normal the trend is toward growing the core business and shedding assets that are not complementary to the main enterprise.

Deconsolidation will become more common, meaning we have likely seen the peak of media conglomerates.
- Consumers will continue to be in the driver's seat in regard to consumption options, and will access and engage content whenever and wherever they want. The smart phone is quickly emerging as the primary media reception technology for most consumers, as well as the primary means of access to the Internet and other digital platforms. Consumers will still value their home media systems with big-screen systems and theater-quality audio, but when away from home the smart phone will be the appliance to connect to the digital world.

DIRECTIONS FOR NEW RESEARCH

With the media economy experiencing ongoing transformation while at the same time trying to determine the realities of "the new normal," there is no doubt research will play an increasingly important role in the 21st century. Research from both public and private sectors will be needed to understand the media economy, to recognize new patterns and trends, to test new theories and hypotheses, to evaluate new business models, and to understand changing patterns and behaviors among consumers.

Here are a few propositions regarding directions for new research and collaboration in the media economy:

- Research on the media economy must be examined as part of the broader social system involving economics, regulation, globalization, technology, and demographics. This opens the door for interdisciplinary research with other fields, including but not limited to fields like political science, anthropology, sociology, engineering, and law.
- Research will be forced to become broader in scope, yet generating more detail in terms of data analysis and results. Media companies will need to invest more money in research in order to maintain a competitive position in a crowded and highly fragmented marketplace. Collaboration with academic partners could produce high-quality, affordable research that could benefit both parties.
- Research must be conducted using multiple levels of analysis ranging from the global to the individual level, and must develop new theoretical orientations and methodological tools. Researchers must take risks and explore new avenues of inquiry,

and not be bound by old models and old methods of conducting research.

- Research on the media economy would be better suited examining broader areas of interest such as content, distribution, and search rather than outdated labels of publishing, broadcasting, and entertainment. Not only would such initiatives be more appropriate, but they would also consider the realities of the marketplace.

The agenda for possible research on the media economy is both wide and daunting. Scholars and industry researchers can build on the foundation of previous work from the past 60 years, while exploring new paths. The opportunity for better collaboration between industry and academe has probably never been greater. At a time when the media industries are suffering financially, the ability to engage in projects with academic partners could open many new doors.

SUMMARY

This final chapter has attempted to provide a summary and synthesis of many of the ideas expressed in *The Media Economy*. First, the chapter reviewed the state of knowledge on the media economy, offering a set of propositions on what we know. Second, the chapter provided a brief discussion on the transformation of the media economy, recognizing that the transformation process is an ongoing phenomenon that may never be complete. Third, the chapter investigated the concept of "the new normal" and attempted to evaluate what the new normal means to the media economy. The final section of the chapter looked at directions for future research, offering yet another set of propositions related to this topic with the hope of spurring ideas and investigations of some of the ideas mentioned.

It is the author's hope that *The Media Economy* has offered some new ideas and new insights to you, the reader, on how to understand and analyze the economic activities of the media industries and their part of a larger, holistic framework identified as the media economy. In particular, I would welcome you to share your own thoughts, insights, and continuing discussion on the evolution of the media economy, by participating in the blog devoted to this topic (at http://themediaeconomy.blogspot.com/) or by following me at http://twitter.com/themediaeconomy.

DISCUSSION QUESTIONS

1. How would you describe the state of knowledge that exists in regard to research on the media economy? What are its strengths, and how could it be improved?

2. What does the chapter mean by stating that the media economy is in transformation? Do you agree or disagree with this idea?

3. What are some of the trends shaping "the new normal" as applied to the media economy? Do you see other examples of a new normal? If so, discuss.

4. The chapter concludes with suggestions for future research. What are some other directions for research you would offer as ideas on how to study the media economy?

REFERENCES

About.com: US economy. (2009). *What are the components of GDP?* Retrieved October 25, 2009, from http://useconomy.about.com/od/grossdomesticproduct/f/GDP_Components. htm

About G-20. (n.d.). Retrieved September 15, 2009, from http://www.g20.org/about_what_ is_g20.aspx

Advertising Age. (2008, December 29). *Media jobs? Depressing.* Retrieved December 31, 2008, from http://adage.com/article?article_id=133496

African-American TV usage and buying power highlighted by Nielsen. (2007, October 18). Retrieved October 21, 2009, from http://en-us.nielsen.com/main/news/news_releases/ 2007/october/african-american_tv

Albarran, A. B. (2002). *Media economics: Understanding markets, industries and concepts* (2nd ed.). Ames, IA: Blackwell.

Albarran, A. B. (2003). U.S. media concentration: The growth of megamedia. In A. Arrese (Ed.), *Empresa informativa y mercados de la comunicacion. Estudios en honor del Prof. Alfonso Nieto Tamargo* (pp. 63–74). [Translation: Management and markets of communication studies for honor of Prof. Alfonso Nieto] Pamplona, Spain: EUNSA.

Albarran, A. B. (2004). Media economics. In J. Downing, D. McQuail, P. Schlesinger, & E. Wartella (Eds.), *Handbook of media studies* (pp. 291–308). Thousand Oaks, CA: Sage.

Albarran, A. B. (2008). Media employment in the United States: An examination of selected industries. *Feedback, 49*(1), 4–12.

Albarran, A. B. (2009). *Management of electronic media* (4th ed.). Belmont, CA: Wadsworth.

Albarran, A. B., & Arrese, A. (2003). *Time and media markets.* Mahwah, NJ: Lawrence Erlbaum.

Albarran, A. B., & Dimmick, J. (1996). Concentration and economies of multiformity in the communication industries. *Journal of Media Economics, 9*(4), 41–50.

Albarran, A. B., & Patrick, W. L. (2005). Models of broadcast station valuation: Review and analysis. *The Journal of Radio Studies, 12*(1), 3–13.

Albarran, A. B., & Porco, J. (1990). Measuring and analyzing diversification of corporations involved in pay cable. *Journal of Media Economics, 3*(2), 3–14.

Albarran, A. B., & Umphrey, D. (1993). An examination of television viewing motivations and program preferences by Hispanics, Blacks, and Whites. *Journal of Broadcasting and Electronic Media, 37*(1), 95–103.

Albarran, A. B., & Umphrey, D. (1994). Television viewing motivations and program preferences among ethnic adults: Results of a longitudinal study. *Southwestern Mass Communication Journal, 10*(1), 65–75.

All-time worldwide box office. (n.d.). Retrieved June 30, 2009, from http://www.imdb.com/boxoffice/alltimegross?region=world-wide

Anderson, C. (2006). *The long tail: Why the future of business is selling less of more.* New York: Hyperion.

Anderson, C. (2009). *Free: The future of a radical price.* New York: Hyperion.

Arbitron, Inc. (2008). *Hispanic radio today.* Retrieved September 1, 2008, from http://www.arbitron.com/downloads/hispanicradiotoday08.pdf

Asian persuasion. (2008, November). Retrieved October 21, 2009, from http://en-us.nielsen.com/main/insights/consumer_insight/issue_12/below_the_topline

Association of American Publishers. (2008). *Industry Statistics 2007.* Retrieved October 8, 2009, from http://www.publishers.org/main/IndustryStats/indStats_02.htm

Bad news for some. (2009, June 6). *The Economist,* p. 37.

Bagdikian, B. (2004). *The new media monopoly.* Boston: Beacon Press.

Bain, J. S. (1959). *Industrial organization.* New York: Wiley.

Bates, Benjamin J. (1993). Concentration in local television markets. *Journal of Media Economics,* 6(1), 3–22.

Bates, B. J., & Chambers, T. (1999). The economic basis for radio deregulation. *Journal of Media Economics,* 12(1), 19–34.

Becker, L. (1992). Finding work for graduates was more difficult in 1990. *Journalism Educator,* 47(2), 65–73.

Becker, L., Lauf, E., & Lowrey, W. (1999). Differential employment rates in the journalism and mass communication labor force based on gender, race, and ethnicity: Exploring the impact of affirmative action. *Journalism & Mass Communication Quarterly,* 76(4), 631–645.

Berryman, B. (2004). Review of radio studies teaching: From on-air to the Web: Redefining the radio producer. *Radio Journal: International Studies in Broadcast & Audio Media,* 2(2), 118–120.

BIA's the Kelsey Group forecasts. (2009, February 24). Retrieved November 11, 2009, from http://www.reuters.com/article/pressRelease/idUS181215+24-Feb-2009+PRN20090224

Burgess, J., & Green, J. (2009). *YouTube: Online video and participatory culture.* Malden, MA: Polity.

Busterna, J. C. (1988). Welfare economics and media performance. *Journal of Media Economics,* 1(1), 75–88.

Central Intelligence Agency. (2009a). *The world factbook.* Retrieved October 17, 2009, from https://www.cia.gov/library/publications/the-world-factbook

Central Intelligence Agency. (2009b). *The world factbook.* Retrieved November 13, 2009, from https://www.cia.gov/library/publications/the-world-factbook

Chakravartty, P., & Sarikakis, K. (2006). *Media policy and globalization.* New York: Palgrave Macmillan.

Chan-Olmsted, S. M. (1998). Mergers, acquisitions, and convergence: The strategic alliances of broadcasting, cable television, and telephone services. *The Journal of Media Economics,* 11(3), 33–46.

Chan-Olmsted, S. M., & Albarran, A. B. (1998). A framework for the study of global media economics. In A. B. Albarran & S. M. Chan-Olmsted (Eds.), *Global media economics: Commercialization, concentration, and integration of world media markets* (pp. 3–16). Ames: Iowa State University Press.

Chan-Olmsted, S., & Chang, B. (2003). Diversification strategy of global media conglomerates: Examining its patterns and determinants. *Journal of Media Economics,* 16(4), 213–233.

Chavez's bugbear. (2009, June 27). *The Economist,* p. 45.

Cherry, B. A. (2006). Regulatory and political influences on media management and economics. In A. B. Albarran, S. M. Chan-Olmsted, & M. O. Wirth (Eds.), *Handbook of media management and economics* (pp. 91–111). Mahwah, NJ: Lawrence Erlbaum.

Chipty, T. (2001). Vertical integration, market foreclosure, and consumer welfare in the cable television industry. *American Economic Review, 91*(3), 428–453.

Collins, J., & Litman, B. R. (1984). Regulation of the Canadian cable industry: A comparative analysis. *Telecommunications Policy, 8*(2), 93–106.

Cooper-Chen, A. (2005). *Global entertainment media: Content, audiences, issues.* Mahwah, NJ: Lawrence Erlbaum.

Croteau, D., & Hoynes, W. (2006). *The business of media: Corporate media and the public interest.* Thousand Oaks, CA: Pine Forge.

Datamonitor. (2008a). *Media in China: Industry profile.* New York: Author.

Datamonitor. (2008b). *Media in Germany: Industry profile.* New York: Author.

Datamonitor. (2008c). *Media in India: Industry profile.* New York: Author.

Datamonitor. (2008d). *Media in Japan: Industry profile.* New York: Author.

Datamonitor. (2008e). *Media in the United States: Industry profile.* New York: Author.

Davenport, T. H., & Beck, J. C. (2001). *The attention economy: Understanding the new currency of business.* Boston: Harvard University Press.

Dimmick, J. (2003). *Media competition and coexistence: The theory of the niche.* Mahwah, NJ: Lawrence Erlbaum.

Dimmick, J., McCain, T., & Bolton, T. (1979). Media use and the life span. *American Behavioral Scientist, 23*(1), 7–32.

Dimmick, J., & Rothenbuhler, E. (1984). The theory of the niche: Quantifying competition among media industries. *Journal of Communication, 34*, 103–119.

Dimmick, J., & Wallschlaeger, M. (1986). Measuring corporate diversification: A case study of new media ventures by television network parent companies. *Journal of Broadcasting and Electronic Media, 30*, 1–14.

Downes, L. (2009). *The laws of disruption: Harnessing the new forces that govern life and business in the digital age.* New York: Basic Books.

Dupagne, M. (1994). Testing the relative constancy of mass media expenditures in the United Kingdom. *Journal of Media Economics, 7*(3), 1–14.

Dupagne, M., & Green, R. J. (1996). Revisiting the principle of relative constancy. *Communication Research, 23*(5), 612–635.

Ekelund, R. B., & Hebert, R. F. (1990). *A history of economic theory and method* (3rd ed.). New York: McGraw-Hill.

Ellul, J. (1964). *The technological society.* New York: Alfred A. Knopf.

Entertainment Merchant Association. (2009). *2009 annual report on the home entertainment industry.* Retrieved October 8, 2009, from http://www.entmerch.org/annual_reports.html

Etayo, C., & Hoyos, A. P. (2009). Advertising in Spanish language media. In A. B. Albarran (Ed.), *The handbook of Spanish language media* (pp. 249–265). New York: Routledge.

Fact sheet. (n.d.). Retrieved October 16, 2009, from http://factfinder.census.gov/servlet/ACSSAFFFacts?_event=&geo_id=01000US&_geoContext=01000US&_street=&_county=&_cityTown=&_state=&_zip=&_lang=en&_sse=on&ActiveGeoDiv=&_useEV=&pctxt=fph&pgsl=010&_submenuId=factsheet_1&ds_name=DEC_2000_SAFF&_ci_nbr=null&qr_name=null&reg=&_keyword=&_industry=

Facts on policy. (2006, December 19). Retrieved October 22, 2009, from http://www.hoover.org/research/factsonpolicy/facts/4931661.html

Fan, Q. (2005). Regulatory factors influencing Internet access in Australia and China: A comparative analysis. *Telecommunications Policy, 29*(2–3), 191–203.

Farhi, P. (2006). Under siege. *American Journalism Review, 28*(1), 26–31.

Fassihi, F. (2009, November 6). Revolutionary Guards extend reach to Iran's media. *The Wall Street Journal*, p. A19.

Find HD radio stations near you. (n.d.). Retrieved November 24, 2009, from http://www.ibiquity.com/hd_radio/hdradio_find_a_station

Ford, G. S., & Jackson, J. D. (2000). Preserving free television? Some empirical evidence on the efficacy of must-carry. *Journal of Media Economics, 13*(1), 1–14.

Friedman, T. L. (2005). *The world is flat: A brief history of the twenty-first century.* New York: Farrar, Straus, and Giroux.

Frommer, D. (2009, April 1). *Hulu revenue estimate whacked by a third.* Retrieved November 9, 2009, from http://www.businessinsider.com/hulu-revenue-estimate-whacked-by-a-third-2009-4

Gantchev, D. (2008). The WIPO copyright framework: A basis for business and development. In E. Humphreys (Ed.), *International copyright and intellectual property law* (pp. 93–110). JIBS Research Report Series No. 2008-2. Jonkoping, Sweden: JIBS.

Garnham, N. (1990). *Capitalism and communication: Global culture and the economics of information.* London: Sage.

Gershon, R. A. (2005). The transnationals. In A. Cooper-Chen (Ed.), *Global entertainment media: Content, audiences, issues* (pp. 17–38). Mahwah, NJ: Lawrence Erlbaum.

Giles, R. (1993). Change shapes trends in newspaper management. *Newspaper Research Journal, 14*(2), 32–39.

Goff, D. H. (2002). An assessment of the broadband media strategies of Western European telecoms. In R. G. Picard (Ed.), *Media firms: Structures, operations and performance* (pp. 169–189). Mahwah, NJ: Lawrence Erlbaum.

Gomery, D. (1989). Media economics: Terms of analysis. *Critical Studies in Mass Communication, 6*(2), 43–60.

Gray, J. (1992). *Men are from Mars, women are from Venus.* New York: HarperCollins.

Griffin, J. (2005). The United Kingdom. In A. Cooper-Chen (Ed.), *Global entertainment media: Content, audiences, issues* (pp. 39–58). Mahwah, NJ: Lawrence Erlbaum.

Gutierrez, M. E. (2009). Mexico. In A. B. Albarran (Ed.), *The handbook of Spanish language media* (pp. 34–46). New York: Routledge.

Ha, L., & Ganahl, R. (2007). Webcasting as an emerging global medium and a tripartite framework to analyze emerging media business models. In L. Ha & R. J. Ganahl III (Eds.), *Webcasting worldwide: Business models of an emerging global medium* (pp. 3–27). Mahwah, NJ: Lawrence Erlbaum.

Harwood, K. (1989). A surge in employment. *Feedback, 30*(1), 6–12.

HD radio broadcasting fact sheet. (2009). Retrieved November 24, 2009, from http://www.ibiquity.com/press_room/fast_facts/hd_radio_broadcasting_fact_sheet

HD radio on your iPhone? There's an app for that. (2009). Retrieved November 24, 2009, from http://www.hdradio.com/the_buzz.php?thebuzz=395

Hedges, M. (2009, September 23). *The hurting side of media oversupply.* Retrieved September 25, 2009, from http://www.followthemedia.com/numbers/oversupply23092009.htm

Hilt, M., & Lipschultz, J. (1996). Broadcast newsroom hiring and career preparation. *Journalism & Mass Communication Educator, 51*(1), 36–43.

Hookway, J. (2009, September 14). Web censoring widens across Southeast Asia. *The Wall Street Journal,* p. A10.

Hoover's (2009a). *The DIRECTV Group, Inc.* Retrieved October 8, 2009, from http://premium.hoovers.com/subscribe/co/factsheet.xhtml?ID=ctfkffhhrxhrft

Hoover's (2009b). *DISH Network, Corp.* Retrieved October 8, 2009, from http://premium.hoovers.com/subscribe/co/factsheet.xhtml?ID=cchffxtkftxrcy

Höyer, S. (1968). The political economy of the Norwegian press. *Scandinavian Political Studies, 3*(A3), 85–143.

Interactive Advertising Bureau. (2009a). *IAB Internet advertising revenue report.* Retrieved October 8, 2009, from http://www.iab.net/media/file/IAB_PwC_2008_full_year.pdf

Interactive Advertising Bureau. (2009b). *IAB Internet advertising revenue report.* Retrieved November 9, 2009, from http://www.iab.net/media/file/IAB_PwC_2008_full_year.pdf

International Federation of the Phonographic Industry. (2008). *IFPI digital music report 2008.* Retrieved October 21, 2009, from http://www.ifpi.org/content/library/DMR2008.pdf

International Labour Organization. (2008). *Global employment trends 2008.* Geneva: Author.

International Telecommunications Union. (2009). *Brazil ends 2008 with 10 million broadband subscribers.* Retrieved November 13, 2009, from http://www.itu.int/ITUD/ict/newslog/Brazil+Ends+2008+With+10+Million+Broadband+Subscribers.aspx

Iskold, A. (2007, March 1). *The attention economy: An overview.* Retrieved October 30, 2009, from http://www.readwriteweb.com/archives/attention_economy_overview.php

Jayakar, K., & Waterman, D. (2000). The economics of American theatrical movie exports: An empirical analysis. *Journal of Media Economics, 13*(3), 153–169.

Jung, J. (2004). Acquisition or joint ventures: Foreign market entry strategy of U.S. advertising agencies. *Journal of Media Economics, 17*(1), 35–50.

Keynes, J. M. (1936). *The general theory of employment, interest and money.* London: Macmillan.

King, P., & King, S. (2009). *International economics, globalization, and policy: A reader.* Boston: McGraw-Hill/Irwin.

Kranenburg, H. V., Hagedoorn, J., & Pennings, J. (2004). Measurement of international and product diversification in the publishing industry. *Journal of Media Economics, 17*(2), 87–104.

Lanham, R. A. (2006). *The economics of attention: Style and substance in the age of information.* Chicago: University of Chicago Press.

Lee, C., & Chan-Olmsted, S. M. (2004). Competitive advantage of broadband Internet: A comparative study between South Korea and the United States. *Telecommunications Policy, 28*(9), 649–677.

Li, C., & Bernoff, J. (2008). *Groundswell: Winning in a world transformed by social technologies.* Boston: Harvard Business Press.

Liu, F., & Chan-Olmsted, S. M. (2003). Partnership between the old and the new: Examining the strategic alliances between broadcast television networks and Internet firms in the context of convergence. *The International Journal on Media Management, 5*(1), 47–56.

Lutzhöft, N., & Machill, M. (1999). The economics of French cable systems as reflected in media policy. *Journal of Media Economics, 12*(3), 181–199.

Magazine Publishers of America. (2009). *The magazine handbook: A comprehensive guide 2009/10.* Retrieved October 8, 2009, from http://www.magazine.org/ASSETS/088C8564EB9E4E978A69B183881AEF58/MPA-Handbook-2009.pdf

Mahmud, S. (2007, September 10). *ABC working to create Web distribution platform.* Retrieved February 20, 2008, from http://www.mediaweek.com/mw/news/interactive/article_display.jsp?vnu_content_id=1003637087

Market Research. (2009). *China-Telecoms, mobile, broadband and forecasts.* Retrieved November 13, 2009, from http://www.marketresearch.com/product/display.asp?productid=2270484

Marx, K. (1936). *Capital: A critique of political economy.* New York: The Modern Library.

Marx, K., & Engels, F. (1955). *The Communist manifesto.* New York: Appleton-Century Crofts.

McChesney, R. W. (2000). The political economy of communication and the future of the field. *Media, Culture & Society, 22*(1), 109–116.

McChesney, R. W. (2007). *Communication revolution: Critical junctures and the future of media.* New York: New Press.

McCombs, M. (1972, August). Mass media in the marketplace. *Journalism Monographs, 24.*

McCombs, M., & Nolan, J. (1992). The relative constancy approach to consumer spending for media. *Journal of Media Economics, 5*(2), 43–52.

Micklethwait, J., & Woolridge, A. (2000). *A future perfect: The challenge and hidden promise of globalization.* New York: Crown Books.

Mosco, V. (2009). *The political economy of communication.* Los Angeles: Sage.

Motion Picture Association of America. (2009). *2008 U.S. theatrical market statistics.* Retrieved October 8, 2009, from http://www.mpaa.org/2008%20MPAA%20Theatrical%20Market%20Statistics.pdf

Murph, D. (2008, July 4). *Online TV viewing catching on, traditional TV watching still preferred.* Retrieved November 6, 2009, from http://www.engadgethd.com/2008/07/04/online-tv-viewing-catching-on-traditional-tv-watching-still-pre/

Napoli, P. M. (2003). *Audience economics.* New York: Columbia University Press.

Nash, J. (1950). Equilibrium points in n-person games. *Proceedings of the National Academy of Sciences, 36*(1), 48–49.

National Cable & Telecommunications Association. (2009). *Cable industry revenue, 1996–2008.* Retrieved October 8, 2009, from http://www.ncta.com/Stats/CustomerRevenue.aspx

Negroponte, N. (1996). *Being digital.* New York: Alfred A. Knopf.

Newspaper Association of America. (2009a). *Advertising expenditures.* Retrieved October 8, 2009, from http://www.naa.org/TrendsandNumbers/Advertising-Expenditures.aspx

Newspaper Association of America. (2009b). *Advertising expenditures.* Retrieved November 9, 2009, from http://www.naa.org/TrendsandNumbers/Advertising-Expenditures.aspx

Nielsen Company. (2009, October 15). *2009 media and communications trends: Ways to win in today's challenging economy.* Retrieved November 6, 2009, from http://en-us.nielsen.com/etc/medialib/nielsen_dotcom/en_us/documents/pdf/webinars.Par.33055.File.pdf

Noam, E. M. (2009). *Media ownership and concentration in America.* New York: Oxford University Press.

Noh, G. Y., & Grant, A. (1997). Media functionality and the principle of relative constancy: An explanation of the VCR aberration. *Journal of Media Economics, 10*(3), 17–31.

O'Grady, M. A. (2009, October 26). Argentina's Kirchner targets the press. *The Wall Street Journal,* p. A17.

Organisation for Economic Co-operation and Development. (2008). *Total broadband users by country.* Retrieved November 13, 2009, from http://www.oecd.org/document/54/0,3343,en_2649_34225_38690102_1_1_1_1,00.html

Owers, J., Carveth, R., & Alexander, A. (2004). An introduction to media economics theory and practice. In A. Alexander, J. Owers, C. A. Hollifield, & A. N. Greco (Eds.), *Media economics: Theory and practice* (pp. 3–47). Mahwah, NJ: Lawrence Erlbaum.

Parrillo, V. N. (2009). *Diversity in America.* Thousand Oaks, CA: Pine Forge.

Patterson, M., & Kraut, R. (1998). Internet paradox: A social technology that reduces social involvement and psychological well-being? *American Psychologist, 53,* 1017–1103.

Picard, R. G. (1989). *Media economics.* Newbury Park, CA: Sage.

Picard, R. G. (2001). Effects of recessions on advertising expenditures: An exploratory study of economic downturns in nine developed nations. *Journal of Media Economics, 14*(1), 1–14.

Picard, R. G. (2006). Historical trends and patterns in media economics. In A. B. Albarran, S. M. Chan-Olmsted, & M. O. Wirth (Eds.), *Handbook of media management and economics* (pp. 23–36). Mahwah, NJ: Lawrence Erlbaum.

Picard, R. G., & Gronlund, M. G. (2003). Development and effects of Finnish press subsidies. *Journalism Studies, 4*(1), 105–120.

Porter, M. E. (1980). *Competitive strategy: Techniques for analyzing industries and competitors.* New York: Free Press.

Radio Advertising Bureau. (2009). *Radio revenue trends.* Retrieved October 8, 2009, from http://rab.com/public/pr/yearly.cfm

Ratings winners. (n.d.). Retrieved June 30, 2009, from
http://www.guinnessworldrecords.com/news/2008/02/080228.aspx

Reardon, M. (2008, September 26). *Online TV viewing on the rise.* Retrieved November 6,
2009, from http://news.cnet.com/8301-1023_3-10052220-93.html

Recording Industry Association of America. (2009). *2008 year-end shipment statistics.*
Retrieved October 8, 2009, from http://76.74.24.142/D5664E44-B9F7-69E0-5ABD-
B605F2EB6EF2.pdf

Sanchez-Tabernero, A. (2006). Issues in media globalization. In A. B. Albarran,
S. M. Chan-Olmsted, & M. O. Wirth (Eds.), *Handbook of media management and
economics* (pp. 463–491). Mahwah, NJ: Lawrence Erlbaum.

Scarborough Research. (2009). *The power of the Hispanic consumer online.* Retrieved
March 20, 2009, from http://www.scarborough.com/press_releases/The%20Power%20
of%20the%20Hispanic%20Consumer%20Online%20FINAL%203.19.09.pdf

Shah, D., Schmierbach, M., Hawkins, J., Espino, R., & Donavan, J. (2002). Non-recursive
models of Internet use and community engagement: Questioning whether time spent
online erodes social capital. *Journalism & Mass Communication Quarterly, 79*(4),
964–987.

Sheth, J., & Sisodia, R. (2002). *The rule of three: Surviving and thriving in competitive
markets.* New York: Free Press.

Shirky, C. (2008). *Here comes everybody: The power of organizing without organizations.*
New York: Penguin Press.

Silva, R. C. S. (2005). *Brazil.* In A. Cooper-Chen (Ed.), *Global entertainment media:
Content, audiences, issues* (pp. 183–202). Mahwah, NJ: Lawrence Erlbaum.

Siwek, S. E. (2007). *The true cost of copyright industry piracy to the U.S. economy.*
Retrieved February 5, 2008, from http://www.ipi.org/

Smith, M. R., & Marx, L. (Eds.). (1994). *Does technology drive history? The dilemma of
technological determinism.* Cambridge, MA: MIT Press.

Sohn, S. (2005). Inter-industry and intra-industry competition in satellite broadcasting: A
comparative case study on the United States, Japan, England and France. *Journal of
Media Economics, 18*(3), 167–182.

Sparks, C. (2007). *Globalization, development, and the mass media.* London: Sage.

Speckman, K. (2006). On the rebound. *Quill, 94*(6), 13–14.

Spending your licence fee. (n.d.). Retrieved November 13, 2009, from
http://www.bbc.co.uk/info/licencefee/

Steinfield, C., Bauer, J. M., & Caby, L. (1994). *Telecommunications in transition: Policies,
services and technologies in the European Community.* Thousand Oaks, CA: Sage.

Switched off. (2009, August 8). *The Economist,* pp. 32–33.

Tapscott, D., & Williams, A. D. (2008). *Wikinomics: How mass collaboration changes
everything.* New York: Portfolio.

Television Bureau of Advertising. (2009). *2008 TV ad revenue figures.* Retrieved October 8,
2009, from http://www.tvb.org/rcentral/adrevenuetrack/revenue/2008/
ad_figures_1.asp

Tirole, J. (1988). *The theory of industrial organization.* Cambridge, MA: MIT Press.

Transformation. (n.d.). Retrieved March 3, 2009, from http://www.merriam-webster.
com/dictionary/transformation

TV viewing moves online. (2009, September 8). Retrieved November 6, 2009, from
http://www.conference-board.org/economics/consumerBarometer.cfm

Umphrey, D., & Albarran, A. B. (1993). Using remote control devices: Ethnic and gender
differences. *Mass Communication Review, 20*(3/4), 212–219.

U.S. Census Bureau. (2008). *Internet access revenue for cable and other program
distribution reaches $11 billion.* Retrieved October 17, 2009, from
http://www.census.gov/Press-Release/www/releases/archives/economic_surveys/
009572.html

U.S. Census Bureau. (2009). *Statistical abstract: Media usage and consumer spending: 2001–2011*. Retrieved October 14, 2009, from http://www.census.gov/compendia/statab/

U.S. Copyright Office. (2005, May 25). *Piracy of intellectual property*. Retrieved July 25, 2008, from http://www.copyright.gov/docs/regstat052505.html

Veronis Suhler Stevenson. (2008). *Communications industry forecast*. New York: Author.

Viacom's MTV Networks and BET Networks implement new structure for linear and multiplatform content distribution. (2007, March 1). *The Culvert Chronicles*, p.16. Retrieved February 20, 2008, from ProQuest database.

Vogel, H. L. (2007). *Entertainment industry economics* (7th ed.). New York: Cambridge University Press.

Waterman, D. (1993). A model of vertical integration and economies of scale in information product distribution. *Journal of Media Economics, 6*(3), 23–35.

Waterman, D. (2000). CBS-Viacom and the effects of media mergers: An economic perspective. *Federal Communications Law Journal, 52*(3), 531–550.

What is globalization? (n.d.). Retrieved June 27, 2009, from http://www.globalization101.org/What_is_Globalization.html

Wildman, S. S. (2006). Paradigms and analytical frameworks in modern economics and media economics. In A. B. Albarran, S. M. Chan-Olmsted, & M. O. Wirth (Eds.), *Handbook of media management and economics* (pp. 67–90). Mahwah, NJ: Lawrence Erlbaum.

Wirth, M., & Bloch, H. (1995). Industrial organization theory and media industry analysis. *Journal of Media Economics, 8*(2), 1–15.

Wirth, M., & Wollert, J. A. (1984, Spring). The effects of market structure on television news pricing. *Journal of Broadcasting, 28*, 215–225.

Wolf, M. J. (1999). *The entertainment economy*. New York: Random House.

Wood, W. C. (1986). Consumer spending on the mass media: The principle of relative constancy reconsidered. *Journal of Communication, 36*(2), 39–51.

World Bank. (2009). *World Bank: ICT at a glance. United States*. Retrieved January 9, 2009, from http://devdata.worldbank.org/ict/usa_ict.pdf

World Intellectual Property Organization. (2009). *Understanding copyright and related rights*. Retrieved November 15, 2009, from http://www.wipo.int/freepublications/en/intproperty/909/wipo_pub_909.html

Zhao, H., Kim, S., Suh, T., & Du, J. (2007). Social institutional explanations of global Internet diffusion: A cross-country analysis. *Journal of Global Information Management, 15*(2), 35–55.

Zuckerman, G. (2009, September 11). Dividends, buybacks fall by the wayside. *The Wall Street Journal*, p. C1.

INDEX

Note: *italic* page numbers denote references to figures/tables.